A Worcestershire
Parish at War

A Worcestershire Parish at War

MOLLIE CARNEY

AMBERLEY

To my family

First published 2010

Amberley Publishing Plc
Cirencester Road, Chalford,
Stroud, Gloucestershire, GL6 8PE

www.amberleybooks.com

British Library Cataloguing in Publication Data.
A catalogue record for this book is available from the British Library.

ISBN 978 1 84868 855 1

Typeset in 10pt on 12pt Sabon.
Typesetting and Origination by Amberley Publishing.
Printed in the UK.

Contents

Introduction

We discovered Lower Moor when we were house-hunting. One spring evening, after many months of searching, we saw Bredon View, standing back on Blacksmiths Lane in Moor. It was a hotchpotch of a building, an Edwardian house built around a Victorian cottage with many outbuildings and three large expanses of lawn. The ceiling was a different height in every room. In the larder, hooks were still hanging from the beams for hams and sides of bacon. It was to become our family home for many years to come.

Soon after settling in, I was asked to compile a booklet about the history of the villages for the Pershore Millennium in 1972. I was soon pointed in the direction of shy Miss Alice Gibbs. I was told that she would supply me with all that I needed to know, and indeed she did. The booklet was hastily produced with the Rector's ancient duplicating machine and stapled together to be sold at Fladbury and Moor's celebrations, but I soon found that I was meant for something else. Alice had decided that I would recount her fascinating story.

Alice Gibbs lived at the end of Blacksmiths Lane in her family cottage, Whytes Orchard, with her beloved cat and a radio. Very soon, this shy, elderly lady and I became firm friends. We would spend endless evenings talking about old times. She told me that as a young girl of six in 1905, she came to live in Bredon View after her father, the respected village blacksmith, had redesigned the house from a Victorian cottage into a refined Edwardian villa, with a spacious new blacksmith's shop across the paddock. During those long sunlit evenings, she told me that her beloved mother, Annie, had died when Alice was two and her brother Donald only a few months old. She left behind a grieving husband and a handsome sum of money. With this £3,000, Walter, her father, immediately set about rebuilding the cottage. A few years later, he married Annie's friend, Ellen Wood, who gladly took over the prosperous new Gibbs household.

Alice never forgot her 'little mother', so did not fit into the family life as easily as her brother Donald did. She was a dutiful daughter and a good companion for her stepmother, whose sister's children lived in a nearby village and were constant visitors. Alice did as well as she could. She attended Evesham Grammar School and learned to play the piano well enough to become organist at Moor Church. She became an exquisite needlewoman.

Alice Gibbs directed me to several of her contemporaries, including Major Smyth and Captain Bomford. I spoke to Charlie Clemens, who had played the organ at Fladbury

Church for over forty years. Then there was Mr Bert Hundy, an unbelievable character. His mother had ruled over his father and himself when she ran the two public houses in Fladbury, the famous one being The Chequers Inn.

Miss Ethel Pearson, who lived in Fladbury, told me about her childhood days, as did Mame Mansell, whose father was Shepherd Gould. She told me of wartime schooldays in Fladbury.

I spent several evenings with Selina Wood, who had been in service at Wood Norton when the Master of the Rolls, Lord Swinfen Eady, used it as his holiday home.

I would hurry home after each expedition and translate my scribbled notes before I visited Alice, who would check them. Gradually, we built up a variety of accurate stories. She would always say, knowingly, 'Wait until I have gone.'

Some of this material was included in my first book, *Remember Fladbury and Moor*. It was a social snapshot of ordinary life in the villages between the end of Queen Victoria's reign and the coronation of George V and Mary in 1911. During my research for that book, my heart was touched by the numerous names on Fladbury's War Memorial.

A Worcestershire Parish at War takes another social snapshot, this time during the First World War, which brought about the mass slaughter of the parish's young men. The way of life that I described in my first book changed forever.

When she could no longer manage in her cottage, Alice decided to go into a home to be cared for. I visited her for the last time and she quietly handed over two large faded Boots diaries for 1918-19. They depicted the anxieties and privations the family suffered and their empathy for those who struggled with the twin blows of deprivation and bereavement.

I have included 1919, for it took at least another year before life in the parish regained any normality, partly because of the terrible influenza epidemic that took its toll on my beloved Worcestershire.

The late Mrs Eleanor Savery enthusiastically gave me Fladbury School's journal, which was kept by Mr Bancks, the overworked head teacher, during the war. I was also privileged to work from the Rector's words to his flock, published in the *Fladbury Parish Magazine* during wartime. The late Major Smyth presented me with a photograph album containing the photographs of many of the local boys who served in the Forces, all sent to their heroine Mrs Elizabeth Smyth, who supplied them with cigarettes and comforts during the war; no doubt generously subsidised by her husband Captain Smyth of the Manor House, Fladbury.

I have always had a very soft spot for Alice and Ellen Gibbs. Writing these books has gratified me and I am pleased to introduce them both to a wider audience.

Chapter One

A Call to Arms

Calling upon the household of Walter Gibbs at Bredon View, Lower Moor, in the autumn of 1914, Rector Lawson listened to the youthful Alice Gibbs as she confidently declared, 'Those dreadful Germans won't get here; we'll be alright; we're an island!'

'This war is going to be felt by every man, woman and child in the land,' the Rector sternly remonstrated. How accurate his predictions were.

In May 1914, the reverend gentleman had moved from his position, held since 1908, of Vicar of Pershore – Pershore being a small, lively, forward-looking Georgian town in the heart of the glorious Worcestershire countryside – to become Rector of the parishes of Fladbury, Hill, Moor, Wyre, and Throckmorton.

Robert Lawson was a serious, stern man who did not tolerate much in the way of frivolity among his flock. He denounced the demon drink in all its forms. He tolerated an exchange of views with his parishioners but he preferred his word to be law and disliked being contradicted.

There was little opposition from other religions in his new parish. There was a sprinkling of Nonconformists, whom he disliked. He would often refer to them as 'Gallithumpin Nonconformists'. And since there was also only a hint of papistry, his rule was supreme. There was one wealthy Jew in the parish, but he regularly and generously contributed to church funds – so much so that when his wife died, an elaborate gilded alms dish was presented to Fladbury Church in her memory. Afterwards, it was referred to among the parishioners as 'the brazen bowl'.

His new parish was a mere three miles from Pershore. He moved with his wife and unmarried daughter into the Old Rectory, an imposing Georgian building of over twenty rooms, complete with impressive iron gates. It was one of the finest situations upon the River Avon. The terraced lawns and gardens that ran down to the river were rumoured to have been vineyards in the time of King Henry II.

It needed several servants and two full-time gardeners to run such a gracious home. The Rector had also brought with him, from Pershore, his Assistant Curate, Reverend D.K. Sylvester, who resided at St Catherine's, a small detached house on Blacksmith's Lane in nearby Moor, where the capable Mrs Harvey kept house for him.

Rector Lawson was known for his lengthy sermons; they could sometimes last forty-five minutes. The younger parishioners would sit at the back of the church and creep out of the church door as the Rector climbed the pulpit steps to deliver his sermon.

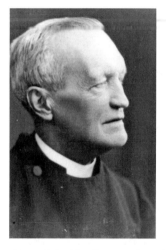
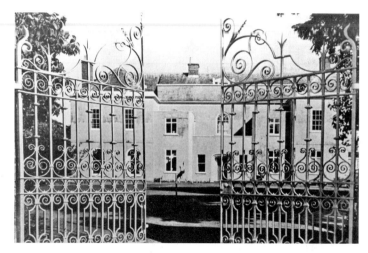

Above left: The Reverend Frederick Lawson.
Above right: The Old Rectory at Fladbury.

Frequently, Head Chorister Mr Arthur would sit with the less-than-angelic choirboys to maintain order during the marathon sermons. So it was with great feeling that the congregation and choir would rise to sing the closing hymn, 'Art Though Weary; Art Thou Languid'.

In the early summer of 1914, life went on in its usual manner in Rector Lawson's parish. No one thought that Lord Asquith's Government would allow Britain to go to war, but on 3 August 1914, when Germany declared war on France and invaded Belgium, threatening clouds gathered over England and spread to the villages of Fladbury and Moor.

On 4 August, when the Germans ignored the British Government's ultimatum and did not withdraw from Belgium, there was no alternative but to declare war on Germany – for England had a longstanding obligation to defend Belgium.

The British Army fired its first bullet on 22 August, at the start of the Battle of Mons. It was the first shot to be fired on the mainland of Europe for 100 years. The British Expeditionary Force spent ten days in France and crossed into Belgium on 21 August. It had amassed 72,000 troops with 300 guns to hold against the German First Army of 135,000 men and 480 guns.

The call went out on 7 August. Lord Horatio Herbert Kitchener, the newly appointed Minister of War, required the first batch of 100,000 volunteers to swell the New Army of six divisions into one of seventy divisions. For the time being, the Government rejected conscription, so the fighting force was based upon 300,000 volunteers.

In the early days of August, seventeen-year-old James Bomford was returning home from Bradfield College's Officer's Training Camp in Borden, near Aldershot, to Springhill Farm, Fladbury, via London. He saw the British Expeditionary Forces of regular and territorial soldiers leaving London on their way to fight in France. By 22 August they had fought their first battle – Mons.

His widowed mother, Janet, ran the large, prosperous farm, assisted by her brother-in-law, Alfred, until James was old enough to take over the reins.

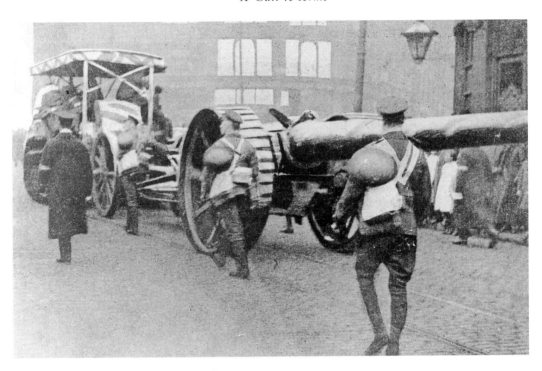

Above and below: Members of the British Expeditionary Force marching through London with military equipment, as seen by Captain James Bomford.

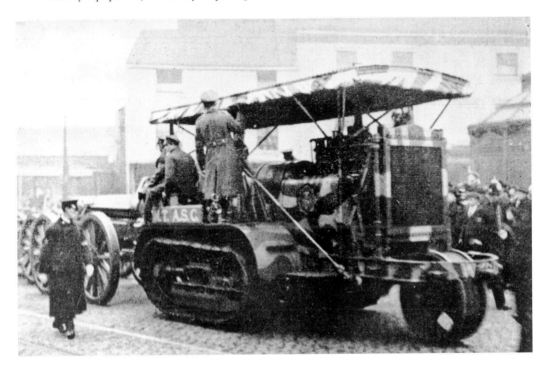

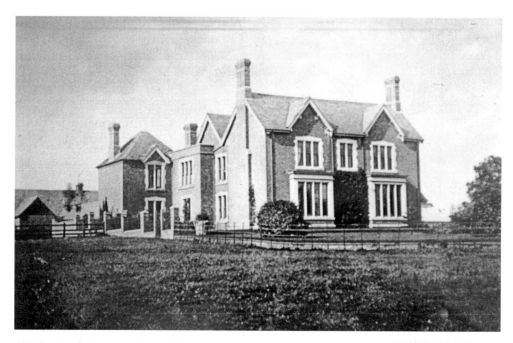

The Bomford's house at Springhill.

The Bomford family was one of the most respected farming families in the Vale of Evesham. Folk said that they were 'buried like cabbages' in the Baptist churchyard at nearby Atch Lench. They were generally known as 'the farming Bomfords', and farmed many thousands of acres in the area. They were well known for their advanced farming methods, especially their early use of farm machinery. Springhill Farm was the main employer in the villages of Fladbury and Moor.

Life in the villages seemed a world away from the terrible stories that came from afar and that threatened to disrupt the tranquillity of their lives – lives that for many years had revolved around 'the ground', i.e. agriculture, horticulture, and village community life. Very few folks ventured out of the parish. The furthest most folk would go was a trip to Evesham, five miles away, to do 'vital' shopping. A trip to Worcester was a rare highlight in their lives. Malvern, twenty miles away, was sometimes the venue of a Sunday school treat. Most people never ventured so far.

Mr John R. H. Smyth, JP, was the editor and chief shareholder of the *Birmingham Post*. Every evening he returned home to the Manor House in Fladbury by train, after a long day in Birmingham. This reserved, stern man was very much aware of the coming conflict.

The Manor House had fourteen bedrooms and was set in fourteen acres. It was the first house in Fladbury to install a telephone. John Smyth had owned an Austin motorcar since 1909, complete with a Union Jack emblazoned on the radiator cap.

He was married to the delightful Elizabeth, known in the parish for her delicious hats and her heart of gold. Before her marriage, she was one of the three musical Stone sisters brought up in Malvern Wells. Her two sisters were close and always came to the Manor House for Christmas. Elizabeth worried a great deal about her younger sister Mary, who was the widow of Adolf Holst – the father of Gustav and in Elizabeth's words, 'that horrid German'. Adolf Holst was always short of money; most of it had had gone into furthering his son's musical career.

Elizabeth was always beautifully dressed and never went out without her hat and gloves. She was devoted to their only child, Montagu, known to all as 'Monty'.

War clouds did not deter her from entertaining the members of the 'Mothers' Meeting' one delightful summer's afternoon in the garden of the Manor House, only a few days before war was declared.

In Fladbury Parish Room on the warm evening of 31 August 1914, Rector Lawson was holding another sort of meeting. No breath of air relieved the heat in the room. The open windows didn't help, for people were packed together outside the room, hoping to hear some of the proceedings. The hushed multitude gathered to listen to Rector Lawson outline the causes that had brought England into a terrible war. 'Causes most powerful, like honour and duty,' they were told. He assured the crowd that 'their rulers' were right to call the country to war. He said that there was 'no other course open which would not have been dishonourable and disgraceful'. With absolute conviction, he told them, 'In this firm belief we can commend our cause to God for help to bear all the strain, the pain, and sorrow that war must bring.'

Sergeant Walker of Evesham, a sergeant from the Worcestershire Regiment, explained the urgent need for men to serve in the New Army for the duration of the war. It was assumed by everyone that the fighting would be sharp but short-lived. A telling speech followed from Mr John Smyth. It was rounded off by Rector Lawson's fervent call for 'an urgent claim upon the manhood of the nation' – a call to arms. The rafters rang with an emotional rendering of 'God Save the King', after which a steady trickle of young men from the parish began to volunteer, urged on by many patriotic young women.

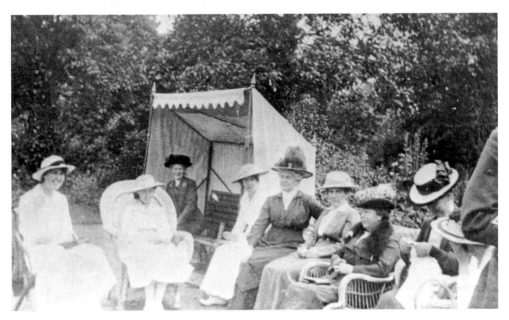

A Mothers' Meeting, August 1914, at the Manor House in Fladbury.

Seeing such a good response from some thirty or forty volunteers, Rector Lawson said, 'God bless the lads!' He then announced that as many of his parishioners as could manage would meet daily in Fladbury Church, after the sounding of the 'Peace Bell' at noon. The rest of his flock were to cease work where they stood for a few minutes of prayer.

As if this was not enough, a list of men already serving in His Majesty's Forces was read out; some of them were already in France or with the fleet at sea.

Thomas Woolloff of Fladbury was in the Navy. His two brothers, George and Charles, were with the Worcestershire Regiment.

Four brothers from Hill Furze – Albert, Frederick, Lionel, and Frank Morris – had joined the Royal Artillery. Arthur Henry Martin, James Martin and Harry Lampitt had enlisted in the Worcestershire Regiment. George K. Stephens from Fladbury Mill was in the Warwickshire Yeomanry, and Samuel Woodward was in the 8th Battalion Worcestershire Regiment. Harry Hilton, the Smyth's chauffeur, joined the Army Service Corps as a motor driver.

In September 1914, Rector Lawson told his flock that it was still difficult for them to realise the meaning of the war; it was difficult to grasp that it meant strife to more than ten million men; and that it had already brought wounds and death to 750,000 fighting men.

'Safe and secure here in Worcestershire,' he told his flock, 'it is not easy to understand even with the aid of pictures in newspapers the vast and horrible desolation which the war has brought to Belgium and France'.

Rector Lawson declared again that he had no doubt that England's rulers were right to call the country to war. He then proceeded to thank God for the willing response by

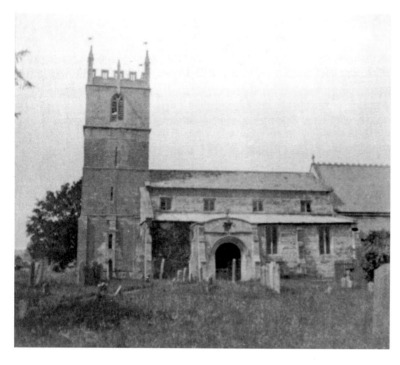

Fladbury Church.

so many young men from the parish who were going to do their duty for their country and their God. For these selfless acts, he felt all his parishioners should rejoice. Swept along by the fierce tide of patriotism, he declared that his flock should 'feel thankful to live in such great times and to be called on to take a true part in them'. Amen.

Two worthy gentlemen sprang into action and planned fortnightly meetings in Fladbury Parish Room, where people could gather to be given information about the progress of the war. They were John Smyth and Mr William James Willis Bund, KC, CBE, JP, DL.

Mr William James Willis Bund was the much-feared, long-serving Chairman of Worcestershire County Council for thirty-three years. He was a powerful, opinionated character who behaved as if he ruled Worcestershire. Many ordinary folk thought that he did.

His family had lived at the Old Manor House in Moor since before the English Civil War. Although he resided in Worcester, he spent a great deal of his time with his unmarried sister Kathleen in Moor, who still resided at the Old Manor House. He was chief benefactor and lay preacher at St Thomas' Chapel of Ease in Moor, where the old and infirm could attend worship.

John Smyth was quiet but equally formidable. He was as used to getting his own way as Mr Bund. He was described by village folk as 'a man of few words, without fear or favour'. However, instead of their usual position of locking antlers, the two men forgot their differences for the good of the community. Things were different now. The country was at war.

Meanwhile, the majority of churchgoers in the parish depended upon the news that the monthly *Fladbury Parish Magazine* brought them. It was written by Rector Lawson

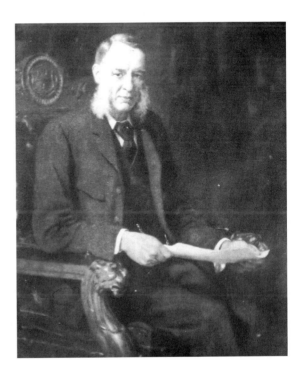

Mr William James Willis Bund KC, CBE, JP, DL.

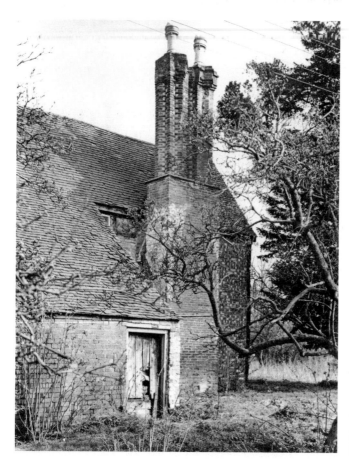

The Old Manor
House, Moor, having fallen
into disrepair.

and distributed to every church member in the parish. As well as 'Hatch, Match and Despatch', there was a 'Roll of Honour' and notes about the men serving in the war. Patriotic gestures continued.

The Sunday school children agreed to donate all the monies they had collected for their annual treat to the Prince of Wales Fund for National Relief.

Fruit was despatched by Mr Eccles of Wyre, famed for his original 'Eccles Tomato Ketchup'.

Mr Owen sent fruit to the brave men on the trawlers engaged in the dangerous job of removing floating mines from the North Sea.

Mr Newman added five tons of apples to be sent to the Navy in the North Sea.

Soon, other names were added to the parish's Roll of Honour: Second Lieutenant James F. Bomford, eighteen years old, was commissioned into the 2/8th Battalion of the Worcestershire Regiment.

Sergeant John Morris of Hill Furze rejoined the Royal Field Artillery, making him the fifth member of one family serving with the forces.

J. W. Lord joined the Birmingham City Corps. H. R. Rowbotham of Moor joined the Public School Corps. Two more names, John Foster and William Harris, represented Throckmorton.

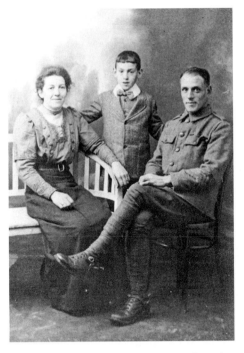

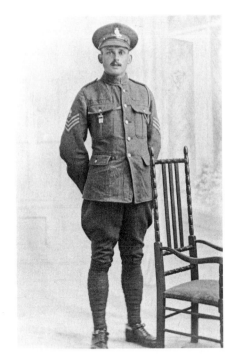

Above left: Fred Morris with his wife and son.

Above right: Frank Morris.

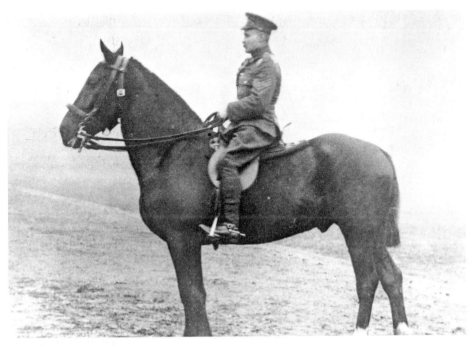

John Morris on horseback.

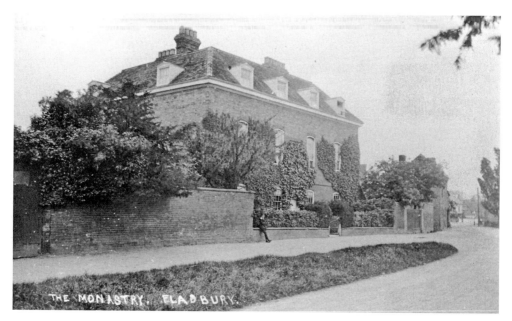

The Monastery, Fladbury.

By late September, after the Battle of Mons and the first Battle of Marne, Rector Lawson sounded a sobering note. Men serving in the Worcestershire Regiment suffered heavy casualties. He announced that Private A. H. Martin was severely wounded in France and had returned home to an English hospital after suffering the loss of his right eye.

Rector Lawson did not falter in his urge to persuade the young men in his flock to volunteer to serve their country. 'Sick or well, wounded or still active in the ranks, prisoner or free, these are the men we honour – those who are *serving.*

'We earnestly hope that the greatness of the need and the grandness of the duty will bring many more of our young men to take their part in this strife for liberty, truth, and honour. There are still many young men, especially in Wyre, who do not seem yet to understand what this great and terrible time means to us all. It is England that Germany wants above all other things to crush.'

At about this time, several refugees from Belgium were welcomed to Fladbury, greatly assisted by John Smyth who secured the temporary use of the large, empty house called The Monastery, opposite the church. It was to house them temporarily. They received many donations of furniture and bedding.

Alongside a large General Committee, there was a House Committee of eight ladies as well as a much-needed Finance Committee of men. Work began immediately to help the Belgian sufferers' temporary stay in the parish as comfortable as possible. Some of the women refugees had to be taught how to cook on a fire range, for many of them were not domesticated.

Naturally, Elizabeth Smyth was among the first to get involved. She had already taken two Belgians as houseguests at the Manor House: Monsieur R. Desart (barrister à Liège) and his wife. They stayed with the Smyths from November 1914 to January 1915.

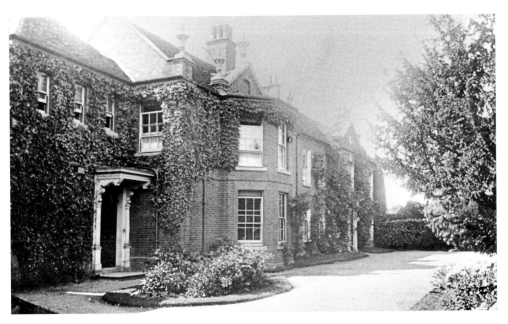

The Manor House, Fladbury.

After the war, many of the original party of Belgians returned home, but some integrated into the local community. One young Belgian woman, Cecille, married Mr Tolley, the butcher in Fladbury. Another of her friends, Berthe, who was evacuated to Scotland, came down to Fladbury to visit Cecille and decided to stay. She went to help Clara Oldham at Manor House Farm in Moor. After the war, she married into the local Roberts family and her husband and her two Belgian brothers took a mere six weeks to build her a house in Moor, which was named Flemish Villa.

Elizabeth Smyth had organised a War Working Party that was to meet on Monday afternoons at the Fladbury Parish Room, where everyone would be welcome and any small contributions were gratefully received.

While many ladies gathered to sew shirts for soldiers, Miss Kathleen Willis Bund of the Old Manor House, Moor organised 'knitting for Tommies in the trenches' at her home.

She was the sister of the formidable William James Willis Bund, but in many ways she was her brother's opposite. She was short, round, and very shy, but had a keen sense of duty. She had mothered both of her brother's children, Penelope and Henry; her brother's wife had long since flown the nest. Despite his protestations, she allowed the Manor House and its gardens to become neglected, believing, without any reason, that she was short of money. She was extremely frugal and saved any old scrap of materials to give out to the village women who came to her sewing circle. She even used brown paper to paper over the cracks in the Manor House's floorboards.

Miss Willis Bund was a deeply religious woman and was never seen without a fine black lace veil over her round, bespectacled face. She even attempted to take Holy Communion wearing her veil. She ran a small library for Moor village people and held the meetings of the Girls Friendly Society at the Old Manor House. It was sometimes difficult for the village girls not to giggle as Miss Willis Bund stood in the open doorway to welcome them inside. Talk about the hooded terror!

It was rumoured that Oliver Cromwell stayed at the Old Manor House in Moor the night before the second Battle of Worcester in 1651. Her brother was considered an authority on the English Civil War and few people dared to contradict him.

Miss Willis Bund selected a talented needlewoman, young Alice Gibbs from Bredon View in Moor, to knit the socks for her nephew, Captain Henry Willis Bund. Miss Willis Bund provided Alice with the wool and she knitted them in the regimental colours – grey, with green and red bands at the tops.

By September 1914, the Roll of Honour was growing, but many more volunteers were needed. The Rector said that he would be glad to hear of others coming forward for their country. He named more of the volunteers:

From Moor
Victor Boulter, 7th Fusiliers
Francis Cole, 7th Fusiliers
Frank Cowley, King's New Army
Albert Pratt, King's New Army
Albert and Arthur Sheward, King's New Army
Edgar J. Pratt, Birmingham Engineers
Richard Turner, King's New Army
Raymond Payne, driver

From Fladbury
Wilfred Lampitt, 7th Fusiliers
W. G. North
Edward Haines, South Wales Borderers
Alfred Haines, Birmingham Engineers
Robert Wagstaff, Thomas and Frank Daniels, Frank Irish, Fred Martin, Victor Smith, James Stevenson, Victor Taylor, Albert Woodward, King's New Army

From Wyre
Hedley Bradley
A. Channell
J.B. Wagstaff

Twenty-five more local lads were on their way to war. Their families bid them a tearful farewell, wondering in their hearts what would become of their dear boys. They were used to a simple rural life and many of them had never ventured a great many miles from home before, never mind 'abroad'.

Meanwhile, the first Battle of Ypres took place in October and November 1914. The Allies and the Germans clashed as both tried to secure the Channel Ports of Dunkirk and Ostend.

Rector Lawson, inspired by the number of Fladbury and Moor lads joining up, suggested that Wyre and Throckmorton should send a few more of their young men to war. 'Surely the parish should share the burden of the war equally?' he wrote.

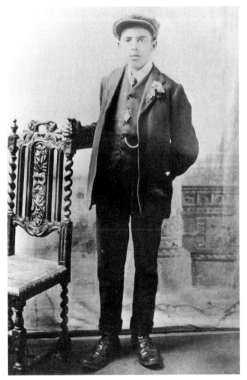

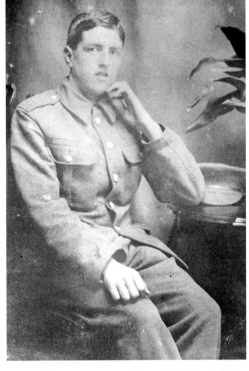

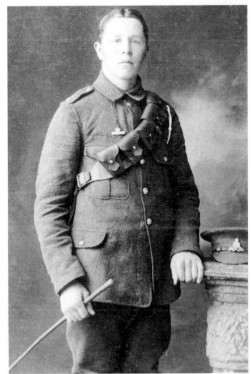

Above left: Albert Sheward, who was killed in action.

Above right: Arthur Sheward.

Right: W. G. North.

Soon every household in the land received this handwritten letter from Downing Street:

Parliamentary Recruiting Committee

12 Downing Street

London SW

November 1914

Dear Sir or Madam,

We desire to draw to your attention to the enclosed form, in which you are asked to state the names of those in your household who are willing to enlist for the war. By filling in and posting the Householders Return without delay, you will render material assistance to the War Office. The names returned will be entered in a Register and the nearest Recruiting Officer will arrange to attest those registered as their services are required.

There has been a generous response to the appeal for men for the New Armies, but the number of recruits, though large, does not nearly meet the Nation's need.

In order to maintain and reinforce our troops abroad and to complete the new Armies that we hope within a few months to throw into the field, we need all the best the Nation can give us of its youth and strength.

If we are to repair as far as may be humanly possible the innumerable wrongs inflicted on our Allies, if we are to avoid for ourselves the ills which they have suffered, if we are to maintain for our children all that we hold dear – honour, freedom, our very life as a Nation – we must fight with the courage and endurance which won for us the struggles of the past.

Every man therefore, who is eligible will ask his conscience whether in this emergency it is not his duty to hold himself ready to enlist in the forces of the crown.

The difficulties and dangers that confront us have never been so great; we await the issue with confidence, relying on the spirit and self-sacrifice of our fellow countrymen to prevail,

We are

Your obedient Servants,

Signed,

Asquith

Bonar Law

Arthur Henderson

Presidents

Fladbury and Moor families began living with the fear of receiving official telegrams. This was the method the Government used to inform the next of kin of front line soldiers and other servicemen about the fate of their nearest and dearest during the war.

In those days, there were only a few private telephones in the parish. There was one public telephone at Fladbury Post Office used by the postmistress whose job it was to distribute the War Office telegrams.

She would send the telegraph boy, who would arrive on his bicycle, knock on the door and hand over the dreaded buff envelope. The envelope was ripped open and with

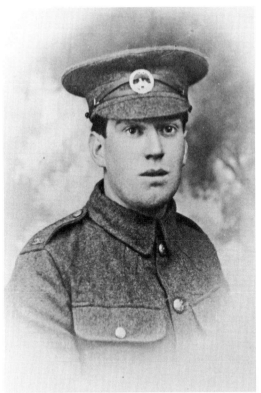
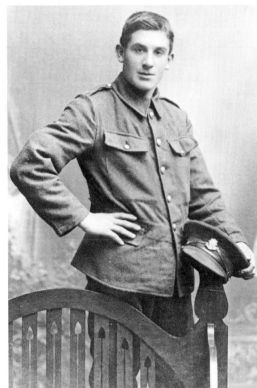

Above left: Ted Haines.

Above right: Victor Smith

terror-filled eyes the householder would scan the statement that would tell them whether their loved one had been wounded, was missing, or was dead.

When the telegraph boy went home, the village children who played by the Post Office would often deliver the telegrams instead. To get their attention, the postmistress would stand by the door and ring a bell. For a local delivery, a child was paid two pennies; sixpence if it was a delivery to Moor, over two miles away. The children naturally enjoyed earning money this way because it sometimes earned them tips as well. They were too young to realise that they were often taking the news of a death and were the messengers of doom to some households.

Early in December 1914, there was a whist drive in Fladbury to raise money for Christmas gifts for men serving the parish; £12 was raised. John Smyth added a considerable sum of money to swell the fund. Cigarettes were supplied to the Armed Forces, but supplies were somewhat erratic and the soldiers were always grateful for other sources of supply. The parcels included cigarettes and pipe lighters, tinned milk, coffee, plum puddings, Oxo, and stationery. Meanwhile, Elizabeth Smyth started to keep a photograph album of all the parish boys serving in the forces. Some of them brought a smile to her lady helpers.

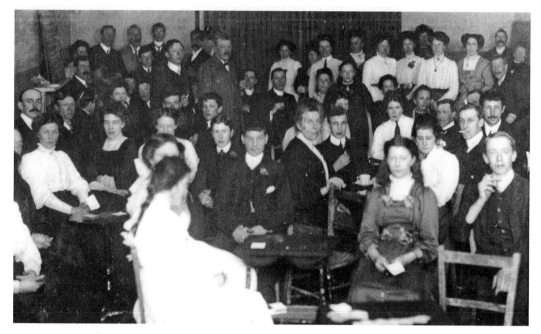

Whist drive, Fladbury.

In May 1915, news began to filter into the British newspapers that the Germans had used chlorine gas in the second battle of Ypres. Although the use of gas had been banned universally, it appeared that to push their campaign out of the doldrums the Germans felt that 'all was fair in love and war'. It took several months before the Allies retaliated. Meanwhile, the fighting men could only defend themselves by holding over their mouths cloth pads soaked in urine.

The growing casualty lists were published in papers like *The Times* and the *Daily Telegraph*. Some issues after major battles like the first Battle of the Somme in 1916, which lingered from July until mid-November, contained over 4,000 names. Many local names appeared on the lists, especially those serving with the Worcestershire Regiment. (After 1917, the officers' names were published, but most of the other ranks were omitted; they appeared in a weekly list published by the Government.)

The local casualties aroused harsh words from the Rector – not about the losses, but about the number of young men who were not volunteering, especially in the village of Wyre.

Rector Lawson wrote in the *Fladbury Parish Magazine*, 'The man who will not be stirred at this time is likely never to deserve the name of a *man*.' He added, for good measure, 'The parents who discourage any son from serving his country are doing him a deep and lasting wrong. To the end of his days on earth there will be honour given to the man who has done his best to serve; if he dies in his country's cause he has shown that he knew how to live!'

It was announced that one of the five serving Morris boys of Hill Furze had been commissioned and was now Lieutenant Lionel Morris.

After the patriotism and pride came the sadness. The *Parish Magazine* informed its readers that Victor C. Taylor was in a critical condition in hospital in Davenport.

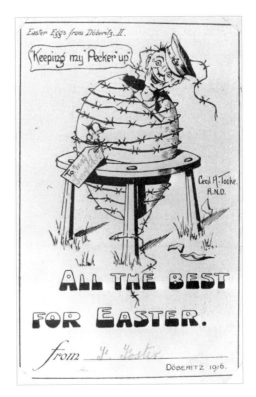

Right: Postcard sent by Fred Foster in 1916 from a German prisoner-of-war camp.

Below left: Basil Smith (centre), who was also taken prisoner of war.

Below right: Fred Foster.

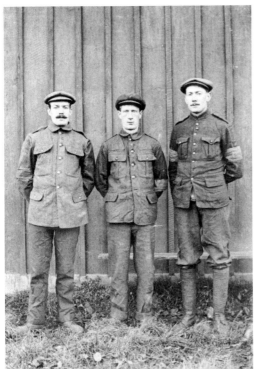

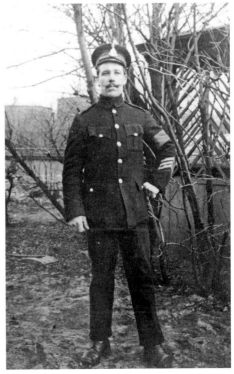

George Woolloff was in hospital in Aberdeen, recovering from wounds to the thigh, Francis Cole of Moor had been shot in the knee and was back home in Moor on leave. Private A. H. Martin had shrapnel in his face and body. Corporal Melville Newman was wounded in the hand. It was announced that Private Fred Foster was a prisoner of war in Germany.

There was further sadness when the parish heard that old Rector Campbell, once the stern patriarch of the parish, had lost his son, Captain Donald Campbell, in Flanders. Donald had spent his childhood in Fladbury. He was not a young man, but he had volunteered to serve his country.

The first Sunday of January 1915 saw the country's churches holding a day of national prayer. A member from every family in the parish took it in turns to go to Fladbury Church and take part in this day of continuous prayer.

The Rector announced that his son-in-law, Major Caldicott, who was in the Calcutta Light Horse Regiment, was coming home from India to take a commission in the Worcestershire Regiment.

The next man from Moor who felt it was his duty to answer Kitchener's call was William Payne. He was more than willing to join the colours and fight for his country, but he was working on the railway and reserved in a 'key' job. The prestigious Great Western Railway employed William in 1908 as a porter at Fladbury Station, for twelve shillings a week. He received a smart uniform and three days holiday a year. He was moved to Evesham, where he spent two years before he was promoted to a station in Kingham.

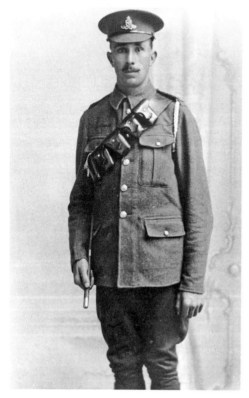

William Payne.

By 1912, he was a porter and guard at the Morton-in-the-Marsh and Shipston Tramway, and was proud to be presented with a green flag.

When the war came, William was at Shipston-upon-Stour. Determined to do his duty, he applied to join Kitchener's Army but had to wait until April 1915, when he was requested to join the Royal Garrison Artillery in Oxford. He joined Colonel Hammersley's 'Lambs', where the men were ranged between eighteen and forty-one years.

The 'Oxford Heavy' battalion soon found themselves at Ypres, where they were 'dug in' for eighteen long, cold, wet weeks. Their trenches were ankle deep in water, despite the rows of wooden duckboards that were supposed to protect their feet.

By June 1916, when the weather began to improve, Will was sitting on a straw bale one day and was pleasantly surprised to read the label on the bale: 'Bomford of Springhill, Worcs.' A despatch rider arrived soon afterwards to tell them all to pack up and be ready to move off in half an hour, ready for action in the first Somme Offensive. Will was to spend three years in France and Belgium before he returned to the railway in 1918. He came home to Worcestershire only twice. On his second leave in January 1918, with deep snow everywhere, he was married at All Saints' Church in Evesham.

In June 1916, during the fierce fighting on the Somme, there was a sad ceremony in Fladbury Churchyard. A new Memorial Cross was dedicated to the young men from the parish who had died on active service.

Other news that month was that Mr Godfrey's charmer of a son, Second Lieutenant Jack Godfrey, attached to the 14th Pioneer Battalion of the Worcestershire Regiment, returned to France after recovering from a gas attack. Gunner Ernest Payne was in a Glasgow Hospital suffering from shell shock. Bombardier Frank Morris was reported wounded. Private Henry Hall was home recovering from an illness contracted in France. The death of Private Harold Farmer, on 30 October in France, was announced, to the deep grief of his parents.

Later, it was reported that Lance-Corporal Oliver Woolloff would no longer return home to his wife and young children, or return to work at the Manor House. He was killed in France on 16 November, just before he was due for home leave, during one of the last battles on the Somme. It was a further devastating blow for the Woolloff family. Oliver was the third member of the family to give his life for his country.

The Rector heard from his former curate, Reverend Sylvester, who was in France suffering from trench fever. The Rector recorded, 'Many of our soldiers in France were suffering from 'Trench foot' and 'Trench fever', including Gunner George Payne, Edward Haines and Driver Alfred Cole'.

He went on to explain that trench foot was caused by prolonged cold, wet conditions. Trench fever, meanwhile, was an infectious disease. Patients suffered from headaches, fever, pain in the limbs, skin rashes, and mild infections of the eyes. He described shell shock as 'the various forms of mental disorder exhibited by soldiers after heavy bombardments or the shock of an explosion'.

Some Austrian prisoners of war were released on parole to work on the farms in the Vale of Evesham, but not all the farmers were keen on this form of labour.

In Fladbury, John Smyth was turning sixty. He felt that he should be doing more than editing the *Birmingham Post* for the duration of the war. In his youth, he had joined the Warwickshire Yeomanry, so he offered his services once more and was made a captain in July 1915. At first, he was put in charge of guarding railways, ammunition dumps, and the Atlantic cable at Avonmouth docks.

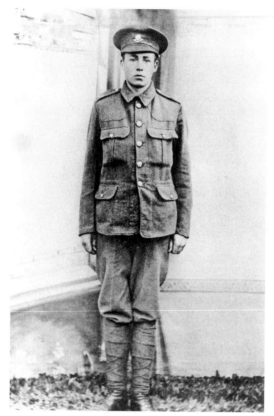

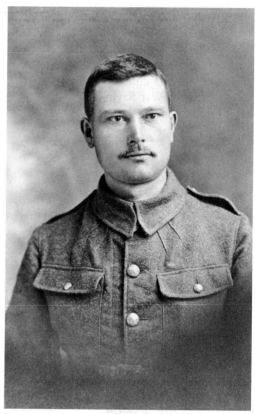

Above left: Harold Farmer.

Above right: Oliver Woolloff.

Finally, he was appointed the Commandant of a prisoner-of-war camp near Grantham in Lincolnshire. He continued in this job until an accident in June 1917. He was cycling back from visiting the prisoners working in a nearby quarry when he was thrown from his machine, which must have hit a large stone. He broke his thigh and damaged his right shoulder and hand. This resulted in his hospitalisation for nine weeks at Harrowby Camp Hospital. Elizabeth took their son Monty and the nurse to stay at the George Hotel in Grantham, so that they could be near to him.

After a lengthy stay in hospital, he was discharged, on crutches, back to the Manor House in Fladbury. The Smyths continued to generously support the sending of Christmas parcels to the men of the parish on active service. The annual whist drive, held in December, made a record sum of £30. Captain Smyth always added a further £25.

Early in 1917, the first death in action to befall Wyre was reported when Gunner Albert Bradley was killed in France by a shell. It was also reported that Private W. Winkett had left for France.

Rector Lawson suffered in his own way, for he could not rely on other clergymen to help him run his parish. Most of the younger clergymen were padres in the Army and Navy. Clergy under the age of fifty-one were frequently asked by their bishops to volunteer for non-combatant duties such as stretcher-bearing.

The formation of a War Savings Association in the parish was a patriotic gesture, but it was perhaps a tad too optimistic. The Rector said that it applied to every man, woman, and child, who were all requested to lend some money to the country by taking out War Savings Certificates. The more money people lent, the sooner the war would be won, they were told. If anyone had £5 to spare, they could take out a war loan. The committee included members of the New Sick Benefit Club, including Mr P. J. Woodward, Mr W. Izod, Sam Pearson, and James Sheward. Mr Godfrey was the treasurer and Miss Lawson, the Rector's daughter, was to be the Secretary.

The schoolchildren were encouraged to donate pennies and sixpences until the money could be converted into a certificate costing 15s 6d, with the British Empire as security. Because the nation needed the money for longer than a year, the interest for the first year was only three pennies. After five years, the certificate would be worth £1. Mr Godfrey generously offered the first 100 subscribers a two-shilling start on their second certificate.

In the spring of 1917, because of severe labour shortages, the Government began to use German prisoners of war to work on the land. Many were sent to the Vale of Evesham to work on 'the ground' and there were several prisoner-of-war camps around

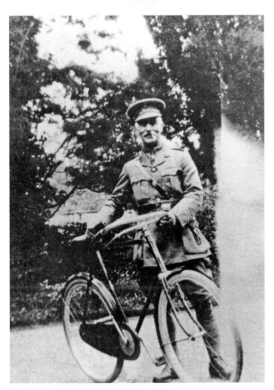
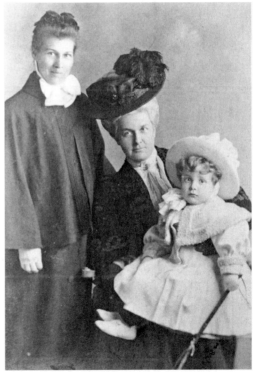

Above left: Captain John Smyth.

Above right: Elizabeth Smyth, with Monty and his nurse.

the parish. The Prussian prisoners lived at a camp at Craycombe, and they would goose step their way to work. Local people thought the powerfully built Prussians were not as nice or as hardworking as the Austrians in Pershore. Most people preferred the easygoing Bavarians at nearby Peopleton. At first the prisoners were escorted under guard to their place of work, but eventually this rule was relaxed and towards the end of the war, the prisoners appeared to be almost as free as the local agricultural workforce.

The German prisoners of war at Pershore sometimes got themselves to and from work without guards, and it was no surprise to see young Jesse Cotterill from Moor shepherding the burly Prussians from the Craycombe encampment to Oldham's Manor Farm in Moor. It was hilarious to see a group of tall, upright Prussians marching along the lane with young Jesse skipping along to keep up with them.

Several of the Germans were indebted to the kindliness of many of the local women, who would take pity on their meagre lunch of a couple of carrots or swedes and exchange them for something more substantial. It was never far from the women's minds that their own sons could be receiving kindness of a similar nature from a farmer's wife in Germany. Many of the Germans acquired a Worcestershire accent when they began to speak English.

It was a most welcome relief when the USA entered the war in April 1917. Several million fighting men were expected from across the Atlantic to join the Allies in their fight against the foe.

Later in the year, news of the Third Battle of Ypres, also known as the Battle of Passchendaele, started to filter through. The troops fought from October to November

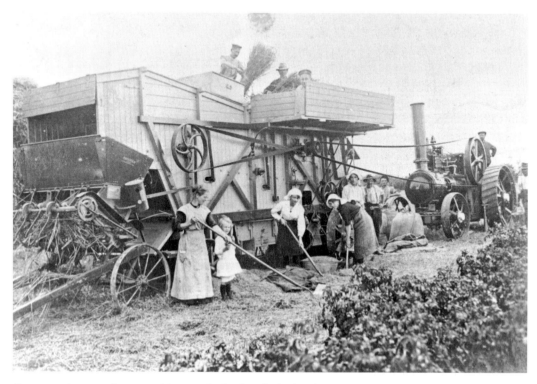

German prisoners of war working on the land with the locals.

1917. News of the battles brought to many hearts the cold fear of a visit from the telegram boy.

It was reported that Corporal Hunt, who won the Military Medal, was making good progress from his shrapnel wounds; Private J. B. Wagstaff was still missing; and Sergeant W. G. Foster was reported wounded.

Neither England nor Germany had given much thought to their ability to feed people during a long conflict. It would play a major part in determining the victor. British scientists, it seemed, held more advanced views on nutrition than the Germans at that time. During the conflict, British warships had successfully blocked many German ports, cutting off food supplies. The Germans opened their campaign thinking that the war would be fierce but short. When they were proved wrong, the Germans found that the satisfactory feeding of their people was just as serious as breaking the power of their enemy forces, both on land and at sea.

Britain had her worries, too. German submarines had sent nearly two million tons of shipping to the bottom of the sea. Until then, the Sugar Commission was the only food control in existence in Britain. A Royal Commission followed it in 1916 for wheat. Fair rationing of food for everyone soon alleviated the fear that the British Isles would be starved into capitulation. By the autumn of 1917, the German food position was

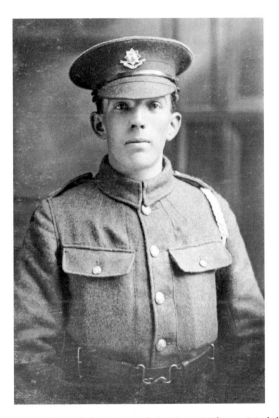 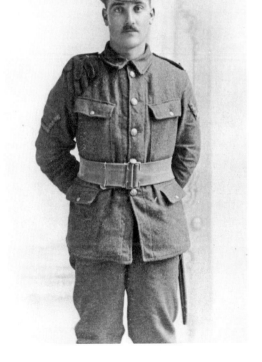

Above left: Corporal C. Hunt, Military Medal.

Above right: Will Foster.

desperate. The armistice with Romania in December temporarily eased the situation, but gradually food shortages became severe.

In autumn 1917, 'food economy' was mooted. It appealed for a reduction in the consumption of bread, flour, meat, and fat. Food imported from America and Denmark was reduced, and Britain became more dependent on her own produce. A new scheme for sugar distribution was announced and every household had to fill in a form obtained from their post office. Wartime restrictions cancelled the annual parish tea for the third time.

On the night of 20 October 1917, the villages of Fladbury and Moor had their first and last experience of the zeppelin menace when eleven were dispersed after a failed raid on the Midlands. The Gibbs family of Bredon View were somewhat perturbed when they were shaken in their beds during the night. Young Donald Gibbs thought there was something wrong with his bed and said so the following morning, but a London relative who was staying with them knowingly informed him, 'It was bombs!' The next day they heard that Walsall had been bombed, with the loss of several lives.

In November 1917, Fladbury learned of the Bolshevik Revolution in Russia and the signing of an armistice between Russia and Germany. This event appeared to increase the power of Britain's enemies, but the arrival of newly trained American troops lessened Great Britain's difficulties and peril.

Other news filtered through. Driver Harvey Pratt had died of his wounds in a hospital in France; Private John Driver had been wounded.

Since the Memorial Cross in Fladbury Churchyard had been dedicated in June 1916, a further fifteen names had been added to the list.

Some of the serving men in the parish had been sent to Italy to fight; it was said that most of them enjoyed the change of scenery and the better climate.

For Christmas 1917, Mrs Elizabeth Smyth reported that 106 parcels had been sent to the soldiers from the parish. Larger parcels were sent to those abroad than to those in the Home Service, and cigarettes were only sent to the discharged. Fladbury had received a large number of letters from the men, expressing thanks for the tangible proof that they had not been forgotten. Many of the boys sent photographs for her to put into the album of photographs that she was making.

She gave a great deal of thought to what was put into the parcels by her band of helpers. She now had a team of knitters, and purchased other items of clothing for 'the boys'.

Several large houses around the parish had opened their doors as hospitals and convalescent homes. Nearby Craycombe House became a convalescent home for officers.

Fladbury Church regularly sent offerings of eggs to the Abbey Manor Hospital near Evesham, and Mrs Haynes-Rudge gratefully received them. The eggs were given as an extra supply of food to some of the badly wounded men. She had offered her home, Abbey Manor, as a fully equipped and staffed hospital in 1915, when thirty patients were received. By 1917, the hospital had nursed 2,500 wounded men. Nearby Chadbury House was acquired as an annexe to the Abbey Manor Hospital, bringing the available accommodation to more than 150 beds.

In January 1918, Private Geoffrey Waters of Moor went to France. Privates Sidney and Lester Foster returned. News came of the award of the Military Cross to Lieutenant

James Bomford after the Battle of Cambrai in November-December 1917, when the British fought a valiant fight but lost most of the ground they had gained.

In eighteen months, Fladbury's war savings had reached a total of £601 2s 6d. This was considered most disappointing. Unfortunately, the regular contributors from Fladbury and Moor were poor. Throckmorton was the shining example, and it was hoped that the rest of the parish would soon follow. Some people had not even completed their first certificates. Mr Godfrey's generous offer of a two-shilling start for the second certificate was still open, but only eighty-two people had managed it. The Rector reminded parishioners that the country needed their savings. He decreed that the war savings total would be published in future in the *Fladbury Parish Chronicle* as a reminder to his flock to save for the nation.

By February 1918, there was a Roll of Honour pinned to Moor's church door with eight names upon it. The Roll at Fladbury bore thirteen names. Life in the villages went on with as much normality as possible. The growing of food was more important than ever.

Friday was the day when the War Working Party met at Mrs Smyth's home in Fladbury. Here, the invited ladies sat around a large table and sewed while Mrs Smyth read aloud to them, usually a short story.

Unfortunately, the lovely lady had what they called a 'fluttery' voice and a tendency to lose her place. She would search the text and whisper, 'There, there, I'd better go on, now where was I ladies?' Despite the stops and starts, most of the ladies enjoyed listening to her melodious voice. The fruits of their labours were sent to the Red Cross Annexe in nearby Chadbury.

In March 1918, the Germans opened their Spring Offensive on the Western Front. It was expected that the parish would have its share of the terrible casualties arising from such heavy fighting.

Rector Lawson reported to his flock that there had been nearly six weeks of tremendous fighting in France and Flanders with forces engaged beyond numbers ever known before, and many losses and injuries. 'It was on this wide battlefield that the war was going to be decided; it is there that our liberty and security must be won,' he said. 'Let no man's heart fail him and let no man forget our brethren and our Allies who fight for us.

'If we try to pray more we can do something very real to help our fighters, and God will give us victory and peace.'

He attempted to describe to his flock the tremendous size of the area on which the battle was being fought – a battlefront of many miles. He suggested that if they could imagine an area from Fladbury to Oxford then they had some idea of the huge size of the long and weary campaign.

The Rector expressed the overwhelming anxiety felt for the many dear lads in France who were striving for their country, and he warned that the Allies might have to retreat further before the pressure of the enemy was halted and turned. He trusted that God would help the soldiers to recapture the ground they had lost, and even to gain more ground after this time of terrible trial. To God, he committed the men, the cause, and the villagers.

The news of the casualties came. Private Henry Fleetwood, who had married a girl from Moor less than a year before, had died of his wounds; Private Ernest Bailey died in France. Three men from Wyre were killed in action.

Many of the Worcester Battalions were in the thick of the action. Privates Driver, Fred Foster, George Pitman, and Harry Boulter of Moor were taken prisoner and were in Germany; Lieutenant Jack Godfrey was in hospital once more, suffering from gas poisoning; Private George Clark was suffering from shell shock; Sapper H. Sollis was invalided at home while his son Private Charles Sollis lay dangerously ill in a hospital in France. Gunner George Payne of Moor was wounded; Private Albert Clarke of Moor returned to France with the Liverpool Scottish Regiment after a spell in hospital; Second Lieutenant G. R. Stephens of Fladbury Mill was reported seriously wounded in France; Private Harold Rose was reported killed; Private George Halls was now a mechanic in the Royal Air Force; Harry Hilton, once chauffeur to the Smyths, had returned to France having witnessed the christening of his son George at Fladbury Church.

The sight of the men from the Abbey Manor and Chadbury Hospitals dressed in their hospital blues – a uniform of deep cornflower blue with a white shirt and a bright red tie – moved many local ladies to raise money for the hospitals. Mrs Henry Rimmell and her daughters from Throckmorton had a jumble sale and raised £16. Mrs Smyth appealed for gifts, which she offered to deliver to the Chadbury Annexe. Many of the serving village boys were in hospital elsewhere – Trooper Edgar Byrd, who had lost his left arm in Palestine, was in an English hospital; Private James Pratt was in hospital in Bath.

By August 1918, the Allied counteroffensive, including tank attacks at Amiens, saw the Germans retreat to the Siegfried Line. Rector Lawson prepared his flock for what he hoped would be the year that victory was in sight. 'We are on the threshold of the greatest and hardest time of this awe inspiring war and greatest because it is the hardest,' he said. 'How magnificently our soldiers "stick it" in spite of all they undergo'.

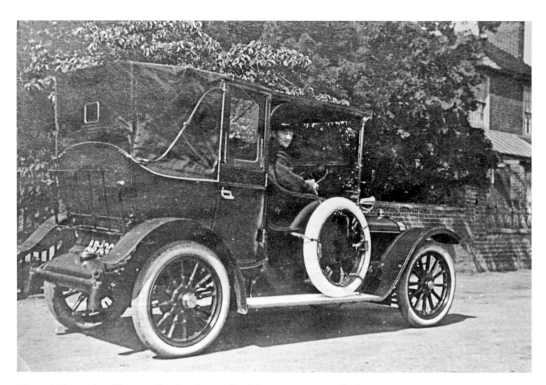

Harry Hilton, chauffeur to the Smyths, at the Manor House in Fladbury.

In 1918, the shortage of coal was making itself felt in the parish. Fladbury School could only be used at night if no heat was required. The possibility of the church not being heated was considered.

In September, the Rector reported that the parish was suffering from a coal shortage. 'We have filled in our Fuel Ration papers and know what is the utmost that we can have. It will be more than they have in France, where no household will get more than 21 cwt for 12 months. In Italy, there is no coal for houses; factories and railways need what there is.'

As the Great War progressed, with the dead, the dying, and the wounded never far from people's minds, the villagers carried on in as normal a way as they could, but with the strong realisation that things would never be the same again.

Preliminary notice of peace had been given on Sunday 10 November, and when the great news came through, everyone knew to assemble in the church.

On 11 November, there was an overflowing congregation for the thanksgiving service at 7.00 pm. 'We must all try to grow in thankfulness, not only with our lips but in our lives,' was the Rector's message of joy.

It was therefore most fitting that the lives of the fallen should be remembered. It was decided that Sunday 29 December 1918 was to be appointed the Day of Remembrance for those who had yielded their lives in the war. Every church in the parish had the Roll of Honour pinned to its door, with all the names of the men who would never return home.

By the end of 1918, many of the valiant fighting men began returning to their native Worcestershire. Gone was the youthful excitement that had pushed them into joining the forces. They were much changed by what they had experienced. Most could not bring themselves to recall any of the horrors that they had endured serving their king and country; so a blanket of silence descended upon the homecoming heroes, a silence that would not be lifted for many years.

The joy and relief at the ending of the war was soon replaced by deep concern as the worldwide influenza epidemic approached the parish. It made its first appearance in the parish in 1918. In December, it was reported that the serious cases seemed to be between persons of eighteen and forty-five years of age. In Wyre, thirty-nine-year-old Harry Sharp died, followed by his brother Sydney, thirty-five. In Fladbury, twenty-three-year-old Florence Cowley died; also May Hughes, aged twenty-seven. The influenza came back to haunt the parish months later, when it was to steal the life of the mother of five gallant soldiers, Mrs Morris of Hill Furze. She had spent the war years anxious for their safety, and now death had deprived her of witnessing their safe homecoming. Two influenza victims, Rose Knight and Alfred Farr, were buried on the same day.

Chapter Two

Fladbury School at War

Fladbury School stood in the shadow of the church, which inevitably greatly influenced the education of the children. The school day began and ended with prayers. Scripture was given pride of place on the school timetable. Invariably, the passages given for dictation and reading practice were from the scriptures.

Occasionally, laughter crept into lessons. After teaching some basic religious truths, Mr Bancks thundered out a question to one small girl, 'Who made your vile body?'

'Air mother made mi bodice but mi Auntie made mi skirt, Sir,' was the reply.

Writing comprised of copying the Lord's Prayer and parts of the Catechism. If that was not enough to painstakingly absorb, there were the Ten Commandments and the Parables lying in wait.

Two months after England declared war on Germany, Fladbury School assembled on 5 October 1914 for the autumn term. Before then, in August, Schoolmaster Henry Bancks had called the children together so that they could be marched up to Fladbury Station to see the brave village boys who had volunteered to fight in the war. Rector Lawson went along with them and when all were gathered on the platform, he said a prayer for the young men.

A great deal had happened during the summer holidays. The Great War had started and many pupils had fathers and brothers who had volunteered and were fighting in France.

'The Monastery', the house opposite Fladbury Church, now housed Belgian refugees and the village children played with the Belgian children with sufficient understanding to have exchanged several English swear words for foreign obscenities. This had not gone down well with their parents, and the children were firmly discouraged from pursuing this form of Anglo-Belgian relationship.

In October, quite a few scholars were absent, for they were still hop-picking. 'Garden work' involved many children and it lasted from April until October. In June, it was strawberry-picking. In July and August, it was pea-picking, plum-picking, and haymaking. Dealing with the apple crop and hop-picking followed this. Parents were constantly advised by the School Attendance Officer to send their children to school; after these visits some of the missing hop-pickers were back in school for a while.

By early November, the teachers experienced great difficulty in being heard, owing to the prevalence of coughs among the young scholars.

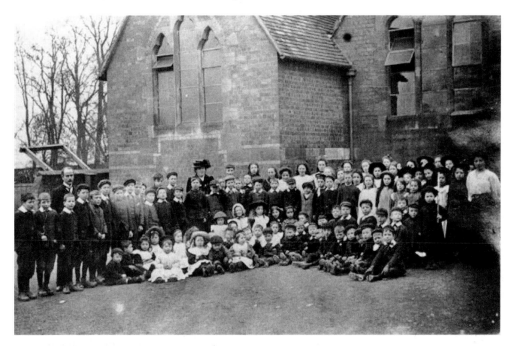

The staff and pupils of Fladbury School.

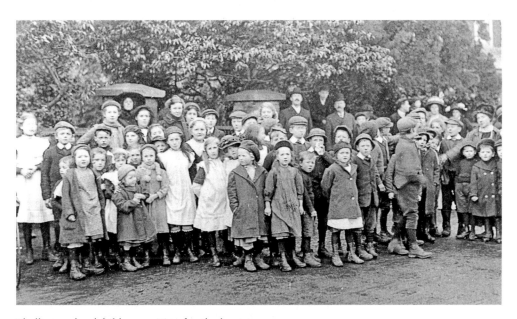

Fladbury schoolchildren waiting for the hunt to pass.

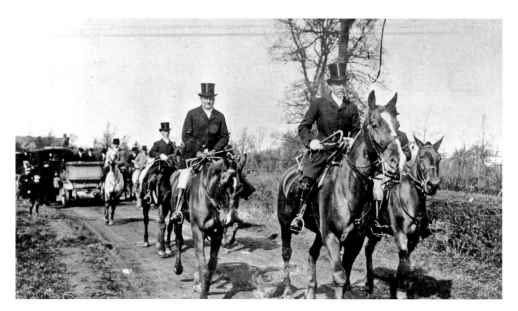

The hunt.

On 9 November, the Attendance Officer returned to explain the Local Authority decision regarding boys over ten years old, who could now participate in employment in agriculture.

Something more exciting happened on 11 November, when 'recreation' was altered, allowing the children to see the Meet of hounds and horses outside Manor House.

On 17 November, the girls were reminded of the war once more, and commenced knitting socks and mittens for soldiers and sailors serving in the forces. In order to help 'forward the work', they were allowed to knit during drawing lessons and throughout their sewing classes. By 27 November, the following articles were forwarded to a Mrs Brauston of Gordon Square, London: two six-foot scarves, three pairs of socks, three pairs of mittens, three pairs of cuffs. Mrs Brauston, who arranged the distribution of 'home comforts' to the men on the warships, wrote to Henry Bancks to say that she was 'most impressed' by the workmanship of the Fladbury schoolgirls. 'They could not be better made,' she said, 'beautifully done.' Because of this praise, the girls were allowed special opportunities to complete home comforts for sailors and soldiers, and they did it with great credit. By December, a further five scarves, three pairs of socks, seven pair of mittens, and six pair of cuffs were sent off to a delighted Mrs Brauston.

On 11 January 1915, after the Christmas holidays, the repairs to the broken school window had not been done, which made the room extremely cold. This did not help attendance numbers. Many of the children were off with coughs and colds. Meanwhile, a Miss Frances came to the school to arrange cookery classes for the senior girls.

By 1915, materials had become scarce. In woodwork, one model became the work of two boys; paper and cardboard work was reduced.

Both the head teacher and his wife were a valuable asset to the parish. They had arrived from Carlisle in 1904. Mrs Bancks was an assistant teacher. They earned £120 per annum and lived in the schoolhouse for a nominal rent. They had two sons, Gordon and Norman. Mr

Bancks was also the church organist and for this demanding job, he was paid an additional £12 a year. His wife was an excellent caterer, as was her mother, who lived with them.

The two women regularly begged pairs of spare slippers from village folk, for many of the pupils walked long distances to school and in inclement weather they invariably arrived at school somewhat damp. They would take off their wet shoes and stockings and dry them by the fire, ready for the walk home. On most rainy days, the large brass fireguard in the schoolroom was heavily laden with wet stockings and the hearth was full of drying shoes.

Because of the long distances, some forty pupils stayed in school for dinner. A group of desks were pushed together and a large sheet of calico was spread over them. The kettle was put on the stove and the mugs were placed upon the makeshift table. Here some of the children opened parcels of newspaper to reveal a large crusty loaf. There would be quarrelling among siblings as to who was landed with the middle of the loaf when all the favourite bits like the crusts had gone. The bread was washed down with bottles of cold tea. Some families were given a great wedge of solid bread pudding for their dinner. Other children were more fortunate, with slices of cured ham and hard-boiled eggs. Sometimes, the pungent smell of the frying fat used by some less fortunate families as a spread could be rather offensive to more delicate nostrils, especially when the fire was fiercely burning in the hearth and the atmosphere became warm and stuffy. In very cold weather, Mrs Bancks' mother would bake potatoes in the schoolhouse's oven and provide hot water for drinks.

Washing up and putting away was worked on a rota system; everyone took part. Henry Bancks sometimes despaired of his pupils. Standard 1, he reported, 'found some difficulty in the "first use" of pens'. Standard 3 'presented a few cases of invincibly "dull" pupils!' Beyond very basic abilities, they gave little promise of higher development. An individual's progress depended on more than their fair share of attention; if it was given, other pupils were neglected.

During February 1915, there were a few notable events at the school. The Moor children were kept under observation because of a local case of whooping cough. On St Valentine's Day, Mr Bancks called in the Attendance Officer because of the absenteeism due to 'bird-minding'. On 17 February, the older girls commenced attendance at Evesham Secondary School for cookery lessons – their railway fares were to be refunded during the next term. The large broken school window was repaired in late February. But attendances were still low; the tendency was to keep children away, 'helping on the land'. After the Diocesan Inspection by Reverend Sheard, Mr Bancks was delighted by the report for Fladbury School, in which the Reverend said, 'In Division 4 the children are taught to think. Their work was most satisfactory and intelligent.'

In March 1915, a National Register was compiled. Men and women between the ages of fifteen and sixty-five registered, declaring their occupations. The voluntary system was not bringing in the numbers of fighting men that were required. The Liberals were reluctant to introduce conscription, but in 1915 a coalition Government put Lord Derby in charge of recruitment. He introduced the Derby Scheme, in which men who volunteered would only be recruited when it was necessary. Many married men came forward, because Lord Derby pledged that unmarried men would be called first. But in the end, only 340,000 men were recruited; single men tended not to volunteer. Further effort was needed locally. The idea was to recruit through Local Government channels.

Mr Bancks found himself secretary for the Fladbury District Recruiting Scheme. Scholars and staff helped in the folding and the directing of circulars to every eligible man. Three Upper Standard boys cycled with literature and messages to the head

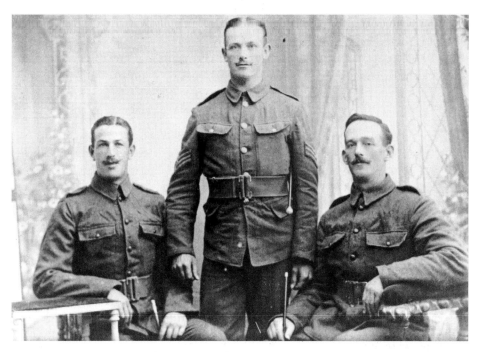

Melville Newman (centre), formerly a pupil of Fladbury School.

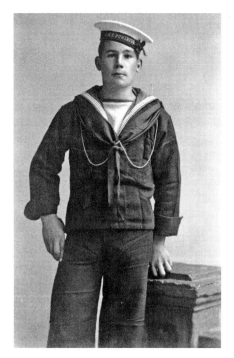
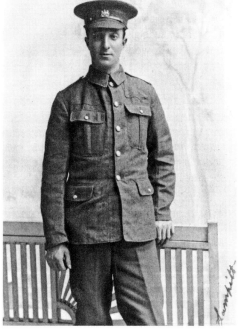

Above left: Percy Pomeroy of HMS *Powerful*, also from Fladbury School.

Above right: Harry Lampitt of Fladbury School.

teachers of neighbouring schools, who helped to distribute the circulars.

He needed considerable time each school day to visit the Central Office in Evesham. He found himself involved in helping with canvassing, not only in his own locality but also the villages of Charlton, Hill Croome, Croome, Earls Croome and Pirton.

He was absent from the school a great deal. Having received many complaints, he did have time to assemble the entire school, in order to warn male pupils against hanging on to the backs of the drays that daily rumbled down the village street outside the school. Mr. Bancks continued to work hard on the Recruiting Scheme. Physical standards were lowered in order to recruit as many men as possible. But despite this tremendous effort, the scheme was still inadequate.

In January 1916, Asquith brought in the Military Service Bill for the conscription of single men, extended to include married men in May. The men refusing military service on grounds of conscience or religion had their objections considered by local tribune.

Mrs Bancks was constantly left in charge of the school. When her husband was home, he spent many hours filling out 'progress' cards and recruitment work.

In June 1915, Mr Bancks compiled a list of twenty-eight 'old boys' who were 'with the Colours'. It started with the name of Percy Pomeroy, one of the four sons of the Robarts' coachman at Craycombe House, now an Officers' Convalescent Home. The Robarts family played a major part in the welfare of the parish before the war.

The school list also included three of the Morris boys, who were with the Royal Field Artillery, as were Victor and John Taylor. Harry and Wilfred Lampitt and Reginald Cowley were in the Grenadier Guards. Victor and John Taylor were in the Royal Field Artillery. Melville Newman was now a sergeant with the 6th Battalion, Worcestershire Regiment. Albert and Samuel Woodward were also in the Worcestershire Regiment. Corporal C. Hunt was listed as gaining a Military Medal.

In July, there was great excitement when an Army biplane landed near the school. The children were allowed to go and have a good look at it before it took off again.

On 20 June 1916, Fladbury School was closed for the day. Children were to join the adults in a sad ceremony in Fladbury Churchyard, where the Bishop of Worcester came to dedicate a Memorial Cross to the memory of the young men who had died on active service in the parish:

H. Barradell
F. Daniels
H. Foster
J. E. Martin
A. H. Sheward
H. B. Sheward
B. Sorrell
J. Taylor
A. S. Woodward
O. Woolloff

In the Autumn of 1916, many children were absent without permission and the Attendance Officer was unable to right the situation. Throughout that summer, attendances were down due to the children working on a heavy fruit crop. After school, most of the children were expected to pick the fruit.

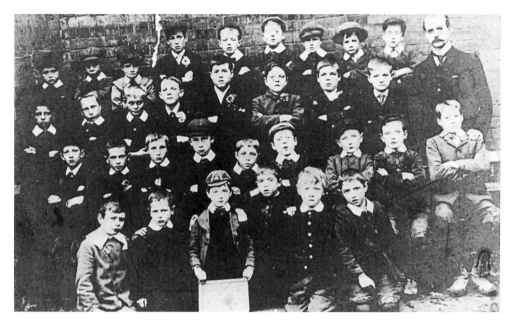

Mr Bancks with a class of boys.

Delicious plums were picked and put into hampers that could hold 56 lb. The hampers were then taken to the railway station by horse-drawn drays to be transported to Birmingham, ready for sale at the markets the following morning.

The school managers were used to the low attendances caused by the children working on the 'ground'. But in October, twenty-six scholars were absent on the afternoon of the Evesham Mop Fair. Some of them had asked permission to go, but this had been refused. The Mop was originally an old hiring fair held every October. By now it was just a country fair, with roundabouts and stalls.

During winter of 1916, the coal shortage was felt. The usual supplier, H. N. Wallis, was unable to send the full order, and stocks were dangerously low. Delivery was unreliable, even with constant pleas from Mr Bancks. Desks were rearranged for pupils to be nearer the stoves. The timetable was revised. Broken windows remained unglazed for many weeks, so heavy curtains were draped across them to control the draughts, though this measure, for extra warmth, took away considerable light.

Henry Bancks found that the repairs to the lavatory pumps had not been completed, despite letters and threats. Repairs to desks and furniture proved difficult, because of the shortage of men and materials.

Building repairs were almost impossible to arrange. When the lavatory walls were damaged by frost and part of the boys' lavatory roof fell in, no help was at hand. The large stove in the main classroom regularly belched smoke, making it necessary to evacuate the children and open all the windows and doors.

Mr Bancks, the poor man, became so exhausted by all this extra work that he was too unwell to remain in the school. He retired to the School House on 14 December, leaving his wife to close the school for Christmas on 23 December 1916. The Christmas holidays were a welcome relief.

It was not until January 1917 that permission was given for a local man to carry out the necessary repairs both inside and outside the school.

In March, heavy snow and sickness greatly reduced the school attendance. During the Easter holidays, the school was scrubbed and the windows were cleaned. Half a ton of coal was received and the drains were examined. Things seemed to be looking up. When school started, however, severe coughs prevented many children from attending. Once again, the sounds of coughing almost drowned the voices of the staff while they attempted to teach.

By March, lessons in manual work were devoted to making a temporary repair to the main stove, which was in a dangerous condition. Between them, Henry Bancks and the senior boys placed a patch of corrugated iron over the offending spot, which made the stove safer to use. An urgent order for a new stove was presented, supported by Mr Walter Gibbs, the Chairman of the Fladbury School Managers, but the chances of getting one were very slim.

In April 1917, it was discovered that several children in Moor who were over five years old were not attending school. Perhaps they were better off, for two Fladbury schoolchildren developed skin infections. The school duly received one tin of disinfectant to wipe over desks and windowsills.

Severe coughs, of an equally infectious nature and sometimes quite violent, developed among the children, making it impossible for the staff to make themselves heard.

Circulars began to appear in the school post, expounding the advantages of poultry keeping. After the Whitsun holidays, an enthusiastic Mr Bancks designed a full-size fowl coup. He planned for its construction to take place during woodwork lessons. He acquired bits of old timber from kindly villagers. Sadly, Mr Bancks' inexperience proved a handicap, so it was a downright failure. This was compounded by the lack of enthusiasm displayed by his workforce. For once, they considered themselves superior to their head teacher in all matters of poultry keeping. In their eyes, he was a 'townie'.

Older scholars were sent leaflets on dealing with eggs, chick growth, and cheap incubators. 'As if any of them needed them!' wrote the disadvantaged Mr Bancks.

At about this time, the Prussian prisoners of war came to nearby Craycombe Farm to establish a prisoner-of-war camp. They were employed to work on the land and farms and were often marched down Fladbury Village Street by a soldier carrying a rifle. Some of the children feared the tall, strutting Prussians; others felt sorry for them and would lean over the school wall and give them a sympathetic smile as they marched past.

Leaflets on crops and seeds were sent by the War Agriculture Committee.

Meanwhile, the Rural League continued to 'send coals to Newcastle'. A circular appeared, encouraging pig keeping. The intricacies were carefully explained to the senior children, who were told to inform their parents of the benefits of keeping pigs.

Most of the parents already knew about the fine intricacies of pig keeping and the fierce competition it aroused between village families. Sunday morning was the sacred time for village men to visiting other pig keepers.

When the pig owner assured the caller, 'He be comin' on well,' they would retire to the kitchen for a jar of cider and some 'pig talk' before the caller tottered on his way to the next pig and the next jar of cider. By the end of the morning it was difficult to know one end of the pig from the other.

As light relief on 25 April 1917, the older girls went to a lecture on 'war cookery' at Fladbury Parish Rooms, accompanied by their teachers. Much useful information was gathered from this practical demonstration of how food economies might be affected.

By May, the number of children with coughs had increased and the coughing fits had become more violent. The parents were asked to watch their children for cases of coughing and tell school staff if sickness followed.

On 4 May, Mary Gale and other members of her family were excluded from school, as they were undoubtedly suffering from whooping cough. A medical certificate confirmed this and the School Medical Officer was informed. The Sanitary Inspector duly arrived and a further ten children were excluded, all suffering from whooping cough. Until the end of June 1917, the school was closed.

July brought better news when one of the teaching staff, Miss Cowley, was married to Corporal J. Huband. The children presented her with a beautiful tea set, as a memento of their kindest regards.

The summer break started on 5 August. It was to be a working holiday until 17 September, because of the fruit crop and hop-picking. Most of the children worked on the land. At least the long holidays provided an opportunity for repairs to the WCs, windows, and pumps. On their return, the children were warned against eating too many beechnuts, as several children had suffered severe vomiting attacks.

In late September, a creditable collection of horse chestnuts – used in the manufacture of munitions – were gathered by the children and two members of staff. Two senior boys were allowed half a day to pack and weigh the horse chestnuts. At the end of November, over eighteen tons of horse chestnuts were despatched by rail. The senior girls were allowed to write and attach the labels. After school, other children would search for fallen walnuts, which were taken home and stored in sealed jars with salt until Christmas.

Early in December, the children saw a series of lantern slides on France and Italy. This helped them visualise where their brothers and fathers were fighting in the war. Meanwhile, the children were asked to bring a large potato to school in an attempt to reduce bread consumption. Mrs Bancks' mother undertook to bake the potatoes in the schoolhouse adjoining the school, so that the children could eat them for dinner instead of bread. Sometimes, as a treat, the children were asked to bring in cocoa and sugar in a mug. Mrs Bancks made this into a hot drink, helping the children to endure the bitterly cold winter weather.

On 16 January 1918, only twenty-two children were present, thanks to very heavy falls of snow. The school was closed for several days until the snowstorm abated and the roads were passable. Colds and coughs made oral work impossible as the shadow of the influenza epidemic was felt across the parish.

Miss Stanton was allowed to catch the early train home, for she was too unwell with influenza to continue to teach. Within days, Mrs Bancks felt unwell and retired to the schoolhouse. For a while, influenza reigned supreme in the parish. It was not surprising; Spanish 'Flu would ultimately kill more people than the Great War.

The newspapers issued guidelines for preventative action, like washing inside the nose each night, and forcing a sneeze night and morning. People were even advised to eat boiled onions and porridge daily, and to take brisk walks. One lady in the parish did the rounds daily with her gardener's boy, carrying buckets of boiled onions to the homes of the sick.

At Fladbury School, the headache of the WCs continued. The flushing had stopped because of a defective tank and obstructions; both pumps were in need of repair. A despairing Henry Bancks was warned that it could be several weeks before the water closets could be attended to. And the coal supply was still unreliable; the coal was promised but not delivered. At one time, only the infants' room fire was lit. There were days when the coal supply was exhausted, when no fires were lit in the school. Little learning could be expected to take place under such conditions. The school nurse warned that an outbreak of measles was imminent.

There were some happy days, however. On 11 March, a Singer sewing machine arrived for 'Sewing Instruction' classes. There was great excitement on 14 March when a Mr Watts and a Mrs Evans visited the school for an hour to instruct the children on the use of the wonderful machine.

In May, Mr Bancks received a 'Mobilization of the Volunteer Force' notice that would require his absence for a couple of days while he marshalled men.

By July 1918, the influenza had returned. It attacked Miss Stanton and several of the children. Mr Bancks and his mother-in-law succumbed to it. It was fortunate that the summer holidays loomed with welcome relief.

After an extended holiday, Fladbury School reopened on 23 September 1918. Mrs Bancks was on compassionate leave in Liverpool, where she nursed her two sons, Gordon and Norman, taken ill with influenza while staying with relatives in the city. They were advised not to travel on medical grounds.

It was just as well, for on 24 September there was a railway strike. The schoolchildren spent several days gathering blackberries. By early October, the supply of blackberries was exhausted and all the teachers were back in school. In late October, the influenza reasserted itself, to the extent that the School Medical Officer closed the school.

The 138 children were sent home after receiving instructions on what to do in the event of an attack of the 'flu. The school was not opened again until the war was over.

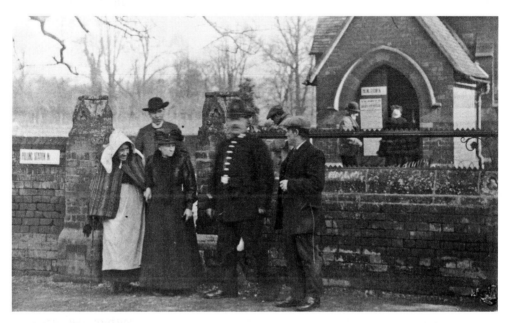

Polling day at Fladbury School.

When the church bells rang out from Fladbury Church on 11 November, many village children ran up to the Rector, who was talking to a group of women outside the Post Office. One child asked him why the bells were ringing and was told that the war was over. There was further excitement when the Rector put his hand in his pocket and took out some silver threepenny bits. He went into the Post Office and bought a Cadbury's 'Dorothy Box of Chocolate Drops' for the children to share.

Fladbury School opened again on 25 November 1918. Because of the disruption to the timetable, the end-of-term examinations were cancelled. The children were far from robust and were unable to concentrate sufficiently. The staff felt debilitated from their recent illnesses and this proved an additional handicap. On 14 December 1918, the school was closed once more and used as a polling booth for the General Election.

The influenza recurred in March 1919. Ten children were ill; a few more were scarcely fit for school. These facts were reported to the Medical Officer and he wrote to advise school closure on the 7 March. The Sanitary Inspector called and took particulars of the cases. Formal instructions to close the school under Article 57 were received from the Medical Officer on 11 March 1919. By that time, Mr Bancks heard that every house in Moor had one or more cases of influenza.

After fifteen years of service to Fladbury School, in 1919 Mr and Mrs Bancks moved to Hampton School near Evesham. Mr Bancks would be missed, for not only was he the head teacher, he was also the organist at Fladbury Church, a churchwarden, and Overseer and Secretary of the local Unionist Association.

During a pleasant social evening in the schoolroom one Wednesday in July 1919, Captain John Smyth presented Mr and Mrs Bancks with a gift from the people of the parish, a cheque for £20 12s 6d.

Past scholars and the present teaching staff gave them an armchair. Mrs Huband, who was also leaving, was presented by Mrs Bancks and Miss Stanton with a travelling watch, a case of silver teaspoons, an oak tray, and an afternoon tea cloth.

In 1919, a new head teacher was appointed to Fladbury School – one Mr Arthur, who was also a trained chorister. In the excitement of the appointment, the school governors omitted to ask Mr Arthur if he played the organ, and wrongly presumed he would replace Mr Bancks in that capacity as well. When Mr Arthur arrived and it was discovered that he did not play the organ, there was great concern. The Rector took over choir practice. Hastily, it was arranged for the young assistant organist at Pershore Abbey, Charlie Clemens, to play at Fladbury for five weeks.

Young Charlie Clemens was tutored by Charles Mason, the organist at Pershore Abbey. Mason was known as 'Quimmey' to his friends, including Edward Elgar. Before Quimmey came to Pershore, he had been assistant organist at Worcester Cathedral, where Elgar would sometimes slide along the organ bench and ask Quimmey what he was playing – and occasionally take over. This was during the time that Elgar was organist at St George's Catholic Church in Worcester. When Quimmey came to Pershore Abbey, the quiet, gentle man taught Charlie Clemens, who was one of his choristers, to play the organ. He would hover over the young boy and was sometimes heard to say, 'You'll never be a credit to me Charles.'

Young Charlie Clemens was booked at Fladbury Church for five weeks. He stayed for forty-two years.

Chapter Three

At Your Service

Selina spent her childhood in Bishampton with her grandparents. Her father died when she was very small and her mother was forced to resume her occupation as a cook, which took her away from home. Selina loved it when her mother came home, for the small family would sit round the kitchen table and her mother would tell tales of Selina's father's life as a coachman to the Duc d'Orléans, the heir to the throne of France whose country seat was Wood Norton Hall, near Evesham. Originally the Duc d'Orléans' uncle, the Duc d'Aumale, had used Wood Norton as a shooting lodge.

On the wall of the family cottage, in pride of place, were two signed portraits of the Duc and his sad and lonely Austrian wife, Duchess Marie. These portraits were presented to Selina's father when he worked among the splendours of the Duc's home. What wondrous tales were told to Selina about life at Wood Norton Hall; it was better than any fairytale. The big house, surrounded by 3,600 acres of land, was like a French château, with ornate black and gold gates leading up to the house. Selina had seen them from the road.

When her father worked there, most of the outdoor staff were English, including Frank Roberts, the chauffeur, and Ben Wasely, the head steward. The indoor staff were mostly French. One French valet married Clara Knight of Fladbury, and she never returned to the village. There were French chefs, although occasionally the infamous 'Queen of Chefs' Rosa Lewis would desert the Cavendish Hotel in London to prepare a meal in Wood Norton for the Duc. She had done this many times for his uncle.

The Duc owned three motorcars, which were among the first in the district, and they were forever breaking down. He drove the cars himself and set a target of four minutes for covering the three miles from his estate at Wood Norton to Evesham Station, where he would catch the London train. Horses and people fled from the noise and dust of the oncoming vehicle. When the Duc drove his cars, local people didn't need telling twice to get out of the way. Sometimes they would see him being driven in a four-in-hand along the old turnpike road with a postillion in front, warning pedestrians with blasts from a post horn. His other means of transport, a white Arab stallion, was kept in his stables. The animal's sole purpose was to take the rider into Evesham to collect the daily newspapers. A less salubrious donkey and cart was sent to Evesham Station daily for a barrel of oysters despatched from London for the kitchen at Wood Norton.

Selina's mother would whisper the bits she didn't want her daughter to hear. This was aggravating for Selina, but she did surmise that domestically 'they' were not happy

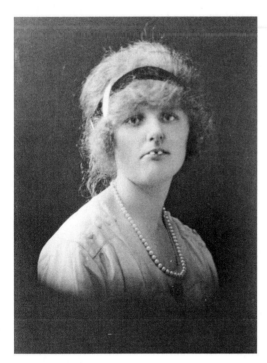

Selina Wood.

at Wood Norton. The Duc had a roving eye and there was talk of him being more than an admirer of the famous singer Dame Nelly Melba. He did seem to spend a great deal of his time in London.

The Duchess had a 'walk' created for her, to while away the hours that she spent on her own. It stretched from Wood Norton to nearby Fladbury and was kept clipped like a lawn. She would spend many hours just walking. When the Duc was at home, he often invited other *émigré* friends for a two-day shoot in his overstocked woods. They would slaughter hundreds of pheasants and rabbits each day. The shoot meant two days of well paid work for local men and youths – sixty beaters would need to be employed for ten guns.

The beaters were paid 2s 6d a day and the refreshments were very good. A hot dinner was cooked and served by the kitchen staff. For some, it was the nearest they would ever get to *haute cuisine*. There was an added bonus for the beaters – they were always given a rabbit to take home with them; their families could have a good meal the next day.

There was always time for a laugh. Instead of, 'A cock pheasant mi' lord!' one raw recruit yelled out, during the firing, 'A cock lord mi' pheasant!'

Selina's mother told her that people didn't consider the Duc d'Orléans a sportsman. In winter, when local folk were short of money, they would trap rabbits and sell them alive at Wood Norton. The rabbits were released into a fenced compound, where the Duc would shoot them at his leisure.

Selina liked to hear about the Duc's menagerie. Her mother said there were fifteen miles of seven-foot-high fencing around the estate. Behind the fencing were all sorts of wild animals. There was a bear pit with two brown bears, a giraffe house, a monkey house, wallabies, and an emu.

People from nearby villages were used to blood-curdling noises coming from his herds of Austrian and Japanese deer at mating time. Most fascinating of all to Selina were tales of what the Duc kept in his museum of stuffed animals, shot during his travels around the world. Selina's father had seen an elephant and a charging lioness in there. He said that there was a leopard and a polar bear, too – and that the ceilings were hung with crocodiles and snakes. Selina was sorry her father had not seen much of the inside of the big house.

Best of all were the stories Selina's mother would tell her was about the royal wedding in 1907, which cost £20,000. It was the marriage of the Duc's sister, Princess Louise of France, to an Italian nobleman who had become a Spanish prince. The local Catholic Church was not grand enough, so a special chapel was built at Wood Norton, mostly using local labour and furnished by Maple's of London.

The King of Spain and his wife, Queen Ena, Queen Victoria's granddaughter, were the principal wedding guests. The Queen of Portugal, who was the Duc's sister, came to stay at Wood Norton Hall for the wedding. Evesham Station saw the arrival of representatives of most of Europe's royalty – including a grand duke from Russia – for the three days of wedding celebrations. Selina's mother said she did not see her husband during the wedding week – he was so busy driving guests about, for they were boarded out all over the countryside. The Earl of Coventry took some guests to stay at Croome Court. Miss Randall, at nearby Chadbury House, had the Spanish Ambassador, the Marquis de Soveral, a close friend of Queen Alexandra. The Squire of Bretforton Manor took more guests.

After the last wedding guests departed, the clearing up commenced. The specially imported wooden floor used in the marquee, built at the front of the house, was given

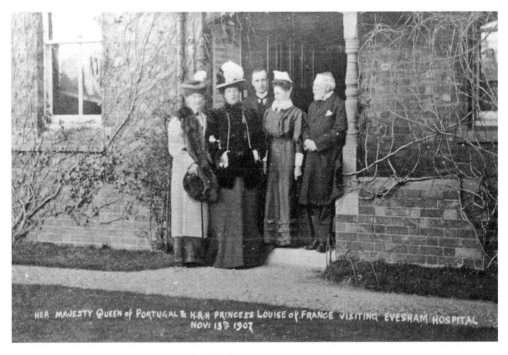

Princess Louise of France and Amélie d'Orléans, Queen consort of Portugal, outside Evesham Cottage Hospital (now demolished).

away to anyone who could collect the wood; likewise, the chapel was dismantled and dispensed. The road to Wood Norton was jammed with lines of humble horses and carts, their owners eager to have some of the beautiful spoils. Evesham Station resumed its former interest in fruit and vegetables, and gradually returned to normal. Everyone agreed that Evesham would never see the likes of it again, and sighed with relief.

It is a grim fact that most of the *crème de le crème* of European royalty who attended the wedding at Wood Norton met ill-fated deaths over the coming years. Few of them died peacefully in their own beds.

These childhood stories lingered in Selina's mind as she became a young woman. She saw the royal portraits on the wall in her home as a proud reminder of past glory. Selina's mother retired from domestic service and came back to live in Bishampton as the First World War cast its shadows over the Vale of Evesham. At fifteen years of age, it was time for Selina to test her wings. Village girls never had a wide choice of career. It was mainly domestic service, but in those days it had its own career structure. To go into service was a good opportunity for a girl to learn a trade, to be well fed, and to be paid a wage.

Many girls aspired to the position of head housemaid – the one in charge of the other housemaids, responsible for keeping the house clean, shiny, and comfortable for the family. Such girls would start work as an under housemaid, doing little work in the front of the house. They worked in the servants' quarters and did the heavy housework. Promotion from fourth to third and then second housemaid was necessary before you became head housemaid.

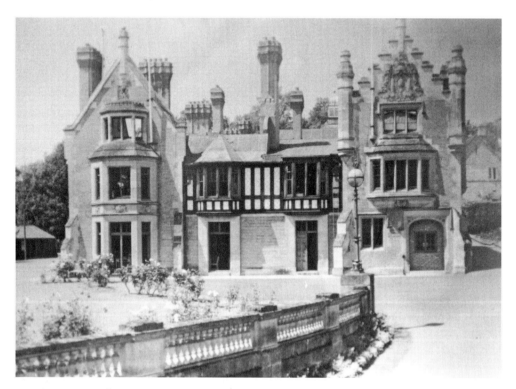

Wood Norton Hall.

In the spring of 1915, Selina's mother came hurrying home to Bishampton with copy of the *Evesham Journal*. On the 'Situations Vacant' page was a vacancy for 'Fourth Housemaid at Wood Norton with the family of Sir Charles Swinfen Eady, Master of the Rolls'. Sir Charles had bought the Estate from the Duc d'Orléans in 1912 and, depending on the judicial year, the family would use Wood Norton during Summer Recess and at Christmas. They had a London home in Hyde Park Gardens and a country home at Weybridge in Surrey.

Dressed in their Sunday best, Selina and her mother walked the seven miles from Bishampton to Wood Norton, where her mother had a word with the head housemaid. The result was that Selina was interviewed and given the position of fourth housemaid, on a salary of £16 a year, to be paid quarterly. The walk back home to Bishampton was a jubilant one.

Selina's uniform had to be made by a seamstress in their village: three print dresses for mornings, with long white aprons and mob caps; and two black dresses for afternoons, with small waist aprons and fancy caps. Her black shoes and stockings were bought from Evesham. Selina was given her mother's brown tin trunk, the one she had used during her own years in service. It was arranged for Selina to start her duties when the Swinfen Eady family came down to Wood Norton for the Summer Recess. She arrived just in time for tea in the servants' hall and felt like a small mouse, hoping no one could see how fast her heart was beating beneath her best dress as she sat down for tea among all those strangers in this great big house. Around her sat the head housemaid, the cook, and the third and second housemaids. The chauffeurs and the two footmen were there, as well as the kitchen maid and the scullery maid.

Everyone was so busy talking that no one noticed new girl Selina, for the large staff had only just been reunited. The butler was busy settling his large family into the staff cottage, not far from the servant's hall. During the family's absence there was only a small indoor staff left at the house. The rest of the staff accompanied the family to London and Weybridge.

Selina shared a bedroom with the scullery maid, along a small landing by the head housemaid's room. The room was sparse. There were two beds and a washstand. Beneath the washstand was a chamber pot – 'only to be used in a dire emergency' Selina was instructed. A corner of the room was curtained off for hanging their clothes and Selina kept the rest of her clothes in her tin trunk. Wood Norton had its own generator, so the room was lit by electricity. Selina was most impressed by her new quarters.

The family comprised of Sir Charles, who was a very stern gentleman; her most ladylike Ladyship, many years younger than her husband; and the children, who Selina thought were nice. Miss Dorothy and Miss Muriel were at home; young Mr Charles was away at Eton. Selina was puzzled when she was told that, because one of the footmen was called Charles, the family and servants addressed young Mr Charles as 'Mr Carol', and they continued to do so for the rest of his life. Servants, she was informed, never spoke, unless their employers spoke to them.

Selina's day began at 6.30 a.m. The scullery maid crept out of their bedroom at 5.30 a.m. to light the kitchen range and put the kettles on for early morning tea. Selina would wash her face and slip on her print dress and mobcap and go down to the kitchen to prepare a tea tray. At 7.00 a.m. prompt, Selina served early morning tea to the 'old girl', as the maids called the head housemaid. This first duty over, her pattern of work began. In the front of the house, cleaning the front doorstep was Selina's responsibility, as was cleaning the entrance hall, the cloakroom, and the long stretch of carpeted passageway that led into the servants' quarters. It all had to be brushed with a dustpan and brush and it seemed to Selina that there were miles of intricate wood panelling that had to be dusted daily. When these tasks were completed, Selina began her duties in the staff quarters. She took time off to go to the servants' hall for her breakfast at 9.00 a.m.

It was usually bacon and eggs or Finnan haddock. The food was good and meat rationing had not yet begun. When it did happen early in 1918, most large country houses had home-reared pigs, hens, and seasonal game and venison to fall back on, as well as their own dairy produce. The Vale of Evesham had a plentiful supply of fruit and vegetables, so food problems were minimal for the wealthy residents.

The servants were fed well and ate their meals after the family had eaten. It was breakfast at 9.00 a.m., luncheon at 1.00 p.m., servants' tea at 4.30 p.m., and a cooked supper at 8.30 p.m.

After breakfast, Selina resumed her burrowing through the staff quarters. She cleaned the male servants' staircase and bathroom, the bedroom of the two footmen, the cook's room, the kitchen maid's room, and the female servants' bathroom. Last but not least, she arrived at the old girl's landing and stairs and the last two bedrooms. The old girl was a Tartar as far as housework was concerned. She supervised the cleaning with an eagle eye and used a white cloth to test the dusting when she went on her rounds. Selina made sure that no speck of dust or trace of fluff lingered in any of the rooms she cleaned. The duster was put on the handrail of the stairs and given a final dust as she made her way down to lunch.

Following lunch, there was some time to draw breath before going up to her room for a wash and to change into her black afternoon uniform. She returned to the servants' hall to lay the table for staff tea at 4.30 p.m. Selina was a little wary of the Scottish cook, who could be a shade temperamental. She had been known to take a footman by the scruff of his neck and march him outside when he came into the hall too early for his meal.

Selina always worked quietly and tried to keep out of the cook's way while she waited for the senior staff to arrive and take their place at the tea table.

As Selina settled down to life in the big house, the old girl allowed her to enter Sir Charles' study every afternoon to attend to the fire. Sir Charles liked old-fashioned country girls; he referred to Selina as 'the gel with the prominent teeth'. He would always thank her courteously on her way out of his study.

From the moment that she closed his study door, Selina often thought that a pair of those new-fangled roller skates might come in handy as she took the copper cans of hot water to the bedrooms before 7.00 p.m. – which was when the family went to their respective rooms to change for dinner. The dinner gong sounded at 7.30 p.m. It was possible to watch the nightly ritual from the backstairs. War or no war, the women, with jewels gleaming on discreetly powdered shoulders and dressed in their finery, descended the grand staircase into the hall. They formed into pairs to enter the dining room. Once the dining room doors were closed, Selina sprang into action. She checked the drawing room fire and then began her tour of the bedrooms. Curtains were drawn and beds turned down. The empty copper hot water cans were removed, washbasins emptied, rinsed, and dried. The ewers were emptied and the crystal drinking water jugs filled. The washstands were wiped over and toilet tables dusted. Selina would cast an expert eye over the room to see that everything was in readiness for its occupant when they retired for the night. If she had missed anything, the old girl would tell her in front of all the staff at supper. Duties over for the day, she returned to the servants' hall for her supper. Once the scullery maid had cleared the table, the hall became their common room.

One night a week, the old girl distributed household linen for patching and darning. Another evening was devoted to sewing cotton bags for the Red Cross. The small bags were filled with dried green moss and packed into boxes. When Selina inquired about their use, she was told to her horror that they were used during operations to soak up the blood at field hospitals near the front line in France. On other evenings they would sit and chat or write letters. On warm summer evenings, Selina took a little stroll in the grounds – but not along the Duchess' walk, for that would take her too near Craycombe House, with its ghost, and Craycombe Farm, with its goose-stepping Prussians. She would walk up the steep slope at the back of the house and have a look at the empty bear pit, with its white-tiled walls, now used as a swimming pool. Selina would sometimes wander around what used to be the Duc d'Orléans' museum and trophy room. She thought it was eerie enough without all those stuffed animals.

On other evenings, some of the maids walked down the drive to talk to the wounded soldiers dressed in their 'hospital blue' uniforms and waiting at the grand ornamental gates. The men walked across from nearby Abbey Manor. Mrs Haynes-Rudge had converted her home into a fully equipped hospital in the early days of the war.

The old girl stayed up pretty late. She sometimes dozed in her chair during the evening. The maids often longed to get to their beds but they had to wait until the old girl had made her final tour around the front of the house to see that all was well before the maids were finally allowed to retire to their beds. Selina filled a jug with water for their washing the following morning and took it up with her when they bade the old girl goodnight.

Respite from domestic duties was well earned but infrequent. The maids had a rota for nights off, about one a week for each girl. Some of them went dancing in Evesham; others would take the train into Worcester to see a show at the Theatre Royal. Selina's excitement knew no bounds when she attended a 'special entertainment' in Fladbury schoolroom given by 'artistes' from leading London theatres, with half the proceeds donated to the Red Cross. Selina returned to Wood Norton full of stories about the 'London Johnnies' she had seen. Evenings like that were few and far between. A more usual treat was a visit to the silent pictures in Swan Lane, Evesham. Time off on Sundays depended on where you were on the rota. Time off after lunch was the best; that meant Selina could pop home to Bishampton. She wouldn't have to be back until 10.00 p.m.

During their summer residence, her Ladyship held several summer tea parties on the lawn for wounded soldiers at nearby Abbey Manor.

On these occasions, Miss Dorothy and Miss Muriel joined their mother to entertain the 'boys in blue'. The family were often joined by members of the Holland Martin family from Overbury Court, the estate on the other side of Bredon Hill. The Holland Martin family were owners of Martins Bank, which was founded in Liverpool early in the nineteenth century. The Holland Martin family were good friends with the Swinfen Eady family and often came to visit.

Selina thought it was very unusual to see Miss Dorothy socialising. When she asked the other maids about her, they said that she must have lost her young man in the war, for she was always so sad and melancholy. She stayed in her room most of the time. When Selina was called to her room, she would find Miss Dorothy lying upon her bed, staring up at the ceiling. She had no wish to be roused from her reverie. Selina was concerned about Miss Dorothy, but she was so formal in her manner that she was

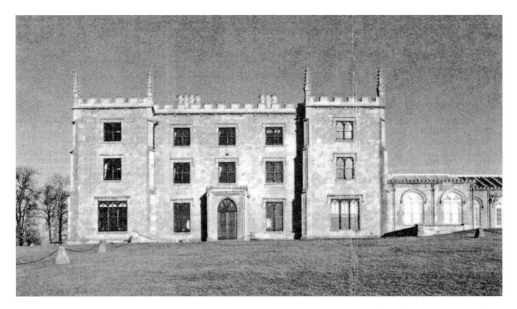

Abbey Manor, near Evesham.

unapproachable. She ate like a bird and refused to see a doctor. One of the older maids said that Miss Dorothy had been a normal sort of a girl before the war. When she had her 'coming out' dance in London, 1,000 guests attended. While she was tidying up, Selina once saw an address book laid open on Miss Dorothy's dressing table. Curiosity got the better of her, and she was shocked to see against many of the names, 'killed' or 'died'. She felt so very sorry for the young woman who had lost the cream of her generation to the war.

Young Miss Muriel was certainly normal. She was still in the schoolroom and took a liking to Selina. Miss Muriel had to go to bed very early. She would demand Selina be sent up to her bedroom to tell her ghost stories. As soon as her Ladyship had made a formal goodnight visit to her daughter, Selina was pressed into telling ghost stories to chill Miss Muriel to sleep. Selina was always careful to say that there were no ghosts at Wood Norton, not like the 'girl in white' at nearby Craycombe House.

The Craycombe ghost was seen by one of the maids, who had arranged a clandestine meeting with her young man in the orangery by the small lake in the grounds. The young couple had just sat down when a young girl in a flowing white dress entered, sat down for a second or two, and then left. She was seen heading for the lake before she vanished from sight. The maids at Craycombe said there was always a certain atmosphere about the place; even the family dogs had their hackles raised at times.

Selina's stomach would tell her that it was approaching suppertime. She would excuse herself and walk gingerly back to the servant's hall. She worried that Miss Muriel would have nightmares after the ghost stories, but it never seemed to bother her and the following evening she would send for Selina for more stories, just like the ones the night before!

Houseguests were a source of interest to the servants, although it made extra work. The footmen used to grumble if a guest was too demanding. One elderly guest had her breakfast taken to her bedroom by a footman. He returned to the servants' hall to say she had several small dogs in her room and that he had to fill numerous bowls scattered about the floor with water.

The 'old girl' was non-too-pleased that one of her bedroom floors was being used in this way. The guest room bell rang again and the footman retraced his steps up the back staircase. He was seen next by the amused maids exercising the guest's dogs in the pouring rain. He returned, soaked to the skin, to rub the dogs down before taking them back to their mistress. He used the most colourful language. The staff eagerly anticipated the departure of such guests.

Autumn came and the time arrived for the family to return to London. Selina never had the chance to see the home in Hyde Park Gardens. She was part of the staff that stayed at Wood Norton Hall, along with the head housemaid, three other housemaids, and the maintenance engineer. The cook, the kitchen maid, and the scullery maid enjoyed their stay in the Worcestershire countryside, but they were never sorry to return to the 'smoke' – to dear old London. The butler and the chauffeur also departed for 'town'. The nursery staff and the two footmen followed. Eventually the remaining servants were alone in the large, empty mansion. But there was no time to spare, for the house and the staff cottages now received their autumnal clean. It was print dresses and mob caps every day and all day.

The engineer dismantled the central heating system while he gave it a service. He checked the generator and cleaned and maintained all the light fittings. The old girl attacked every room with the vigour of all her housemaids put together. Furniture was wiped over with a cloth wrung out in warm water with a touch of vinegar, dried with a soft cloth, and waxed with the old girl's recipe of turpentine, beeswax, and soap. Then it was pushed into the centre of the room and dust-sheeted. All moveable carpets were removed for cleaning. Floors were stripped and re-polished. Grates were cleaned and burnished, and the black iron firebacks were restored to their pristine state, the *fleur-de-lis* once more clearly defined. The ormolu doorknobs were gently restored to their glory. Cobwebs were removed using a long-handled bamboo pole with a soft brush attached. Upholstery was gently brushed free of dust with a hand brush. Gilt picture frames and mirrors were handled in cotton gloves and gently brushed with a camel hairbrush.

The drawing room carpet was fitted, so it was liberally sprinkled with damp, used tea leaves to stop the dust rising when it was hand brushed.

The windows and mirrors were cleaned with chamois leather wrung out in lukewarm water mixed with a drop of vinegar, and then polished with a soft white cloth. Silver gilt doorknobs and fingerplates were rubbed with soft cloths. The Duc d'Orléans' famous bathroom did not escape the cleaning crusade. The green marble walls were washed down, the silver taps were rubbed over, and the silver gilt crown above the shower gleamed. All three washbasins were scoured. Selina could never make out which washbasin was for teeth, hands, or face.

As the days passed, Selina grew allergic to the *fleur-de-lis*, the royal monograms, and the lilies of France. They were everywhere; above every overmantel, on the firebacks, around the electric light switches, and on the light fittings. When you went up the grand staircase, the newel post finials were crowns and the old duc's monogram was woven in gold thread on the silk wall panels. The maids all agreed that you could have too much of a good thing. You could never forget whose house it had been.

After this cleaning marathon, Selina was allowed to go home for a week. During a break in 1918, she met Sergeant Raymond Wood. He was a good, steady man, glad to

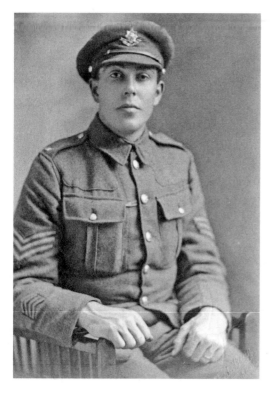

Raymond Wood.

be back in his beloved Worcestershire. He had returned to his widowed mother's home in Peopleton after serving with the Worcestershire Regiment in France and Italy.

Although Raymond was several years older than Selina, the pair got on well together. Selina was introduced to his sisters, Alice and Annie, who often visited their Aunt Adams at nearby Craycombe Farm.

Selina knew Donald Gibbs of Moor. His stepmother Ellen was Raymond's favourite Aunt. Ellen Gibbs and Raymond's mother, Polly Wood, were devoted sisters. Raymond had another brother, John, who was still abroad in Palestine.

Raymond was looking forward to being a civilian. The couple used to take long walks together and talk a great deal as they walked. Selina was a good listener and Raymond would unwind and tell Selina about some of his experiences in the war. Selina was flattered and touched that Raymond would confide in her about his war experiences – most of the men returning confided in no one.

He had volunteered with enthusiasm to join one of the Worcester battalions. Along with several of his friends from home, he was soon sent to a training unit for trench warfare, complete with mock-up trenches. Raymond said that they were nothing like the real thing – they lacked the mud and water up to the ankles and those large, fat, squeaking rats that shared their existence in the trenches. But it was as well the volunteers did not know that at the time.

The recruits had to train to jump across the six-foot-wide trenches with full packs on their backs. If they failed, they dropped eight feet into the trench and were badly winded and out of action for a time. All this was necessary when advancing towards the enemy,

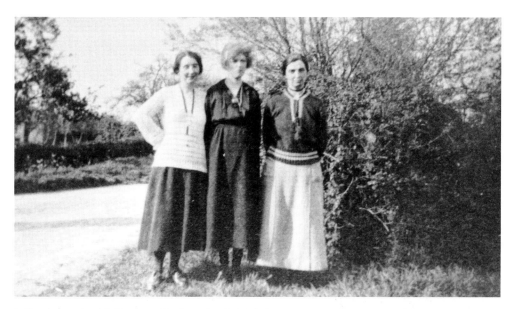

Selina (centre) with Raymond's sister Annie (right).

especially if there were no ladders or duckboards to run across the trenches. They were told how to survive in the trenches. You had to dig the trench deeper than the 'fire step' – where you stood to fire your rifle – perhaps three foot deeper. The trench had to be dug at least six feet deep to protect the head of the soldier from the Snipers. A short, sharp course on the firing ranges followed. Three bulls' eyes and you had passed. Their brief training was completed.

Soon, Raymond's unit was on its way to France. They marched, he thought, to Folkestone, although soldiers were never told where they were going. Conditions were appalling. They had to wait a day and a night before sailing. There were no destroyers to shepherd them across the Channel, which was occupied by German submarines. The troops had a rough passage. They were packed so tightly together on the ship that no man could get to the rail of the ship if he felt sick. After this appalling passage, they were given no time to recover from the voyage; they were hastily herded into trains in Boulogne and transported to headquarters in Étaples.

The first sight of the trenches was a tremendous shock to the men. They were given no warning. The French countryside was quite flat, with a thin layer of top soil over deep chalk that was impossible to drain. The survival tactics taught in England were of no avail in France. If you dug three feet below the 'fire step', water just poured in. You had a choice; have dry feet for a while or stand in eighteen inches of water to protect your head from sniper fire.

The combination of the rain and chalk soil soon became a morass into which bodies and horses just disappeared. The stench of the dead bodies was a smell that you never got used to. Raymond saw some of the tanks that had been brought to France with nothing but their gun turrets sticking out of the mud.

Garrison guns were placed upon caterpillar tracks that spread the weight and were pulled by a team of six carthorses.

When the men walked down the vast warrens of trenches, they caught their sleeves on the wet chalk sides. This mixture, if left on the sleeves of a greatcoat, congealed and was extremely difficult to remove. Some of the old timers wore khaki aprons that gave them some protection. When ground sheet capes arrived, they were a good protection from the sides of the trenches.

Life in the trenches was a mixture of emotions. Men exchanged confidences during the long, anxious wait to go over the top. You had to take what sleep you could in the long burrow of trenches. The green flares bursting in the night sky didn't help. The rats were another hazard. They were fat, aggressive brutes that would run over the men as they lay sleeping. At night, they would squeal at one another and the men would try to bayonet them. Raymond shuddered to imagine what these huge creatures fed upon.

The morning's 'stand to' was soon upon them, then the wait for the barrage of guns to do their job. Then came the 'standstill', which forced prayers into your head. When the whistle sounded, you were on your way over the top, hoping that the fifty yards of barbed wire had been truly flattened and the way made clear for you to advance. At the beginning of the war, the infantry was given the odd tot of rum. Some of his country pals found the going hard. Most were alarmed and bewildered to find themselves miles from home, fighting in a bitter war under conditions they could never have imagined back in Britain. It seemed to Raymond that the 'townies' among the men seemed to cope much better.

Feeling rather small after what she had heard, Selina told Raymond of her weekly task of making green moss packs for field hospitals. His reply did not comfort her. He told her that his close friend Will was hit by shrapnel, which badly damaged his left wrist after an engagement with 'the Hun'. Bleeding profusely, he staunched the bleeding and managed to walk back to the frontline, leaving behind him the dead and the dying and feeling helpless to do anything about it. All the field dressing stations were overwhelmed by the vast number of wounded. Many badly wounded casualties were lying on beds of straw, still awaiting attention. Since Will could walk, he was told to carry on. It was the following day that he found a Casualty Unit that could treat him. It was discovered that he had spinal injuries and a smashed wrist. The following day, he was put on a hospital train to Rouen. Selina was horrified to hear that enemy planes would dive-bomb the British and French hospital trains while the British planes, armed with machine guns, valiantly fought them off. Some wagons had slits in the sides for rifles. Raymond told her that the Germans did not hesitate to bomb Red Cross hospitals. So the Allies had placed German prisoner-of-war camps near the hospitals, which reduced the bombing attacks. The hospitals were usually near railways. Hospital trains full of the wounded were brought as close to the hospitals as possible, from the Casualty Clearing Stations behind the lines. The hospitals were cold, with only primitive heating. Many of the Queen Alexandra's nurses complained of the cold. Selina was relieved to know that Raymond's friend was soon shipped to England, where he spent several months in hospital before being discharged from the army. She was so thankful that Raymond had survived the war and would soon be home for good.

By the time her holiday was over, Selina was most smitten with this nice man and she returned to Wood Norton Hall with a light heart, even though it was time to begin preparations for a large family party expected during the Christmas recess. It was always a very busy Christmas fortnight for the staff. There was little time off, as there were always extra guests. So Selina looked forward to 'a bit of a let up' in mid-January, when everyone would return to London. There were celebrations among the staff when

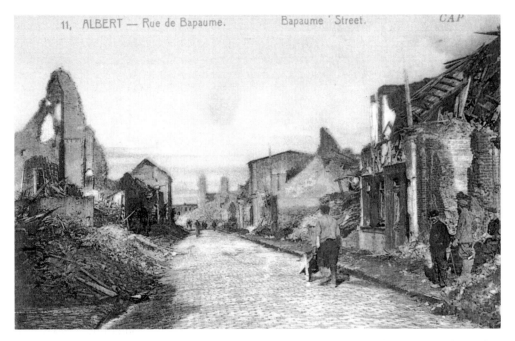

Rue de Bapaume, France. A scene typical of the the destruction witnessed by Raymond Wood's friend Will.

Sir Charles became Lord Swinfen. There was great pride among the staff that their stern but kindly employer had been honoured, but their pleasure and pride soon turned to deep sorrow when he became ill with cancer not long afterwards. He died in 1919.

Wood Norton was up for sale; Selina was no longer needed. The house would never again be used as a home to an aristocratic family. Lord Swinfen's young son Carol became Lord Swinfen. He later married a girl called Mary Aline Mynors Farmar, who was to become the author Mary Wesley. She produced a son and heir, Roger Mynors Swinfen Eady.

Selina and Raymond Wood continued their courtship. Instead of coming home to a land fit for heroes, ex-servicemen found that jobs were not plentiful.

When the officers vacated Craycombe House, it moved once more into private hands. Raymond was glad to take the job of head gardener at Craycombe House. He had two under gardeners and a boy from the village to help him. His position provided him with a staff cottage on the estate. Selina and Raymond were married and moved into their first home together.

Raymond became head gardener to one Mrs Cumming Butler and her widowed mother, Mrs Gresley-Hall, who was the widow of the Bishop of the Uganda Protectorate. She was a most religious lady, prone to falling on her knees and praying at any given moment.

Instead of inviting her friends and acquaintances to meet her for coffee, Mrs Gresley Hall would make arrangements for them to meet and pray together in Fladbury Church. Long before the elderly lady rose to her feet, her companions found themselves running out of prayers and idly made imaginative patterns upon the church ceiling.

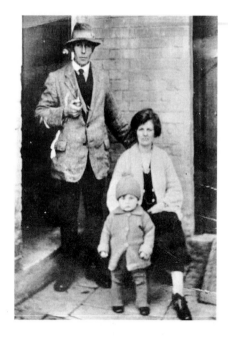

Raymond and Selina Wood with their son Victor at Craycombe House.

Her daughter had a hobby of keeping goats. Alas, Mrs Cumming Butler spent so much time with her beloved goats that she was immune to their odour. She was Chairman of Fladbury Church Council and she invariably finished milking the goats just before she attended the council meetings. Unfortunately her fellow members were not immune to goat odours; the lady's presence caused them to hold their breath awhile.

Despite the religious fervour, there were soon more ghostly goings-on at Craycombe House. Raymond's young assistant Tom was frightened one morning when he found the 'girl in white' sitting in the orangery. He ran to the house to fetch the other gardener's boy and they both saw the ghostly apparition moving out of the orangery, the white dress and her shoe disappearing before their eyes.

One of the braver lodge men would check the big house when the family were away, but his wife would never go with him.

Selina and Raymond went on to have four sons, Norman John, Victor, Stanley, and Bill, who were all born and brought up at Craycombe.

Many years later, the dowager Lady Cobham moved into Craycombe House and was sufficiently annoyed one night to send for Fladbury's village policeman. She complained that she had seen a girl in white leaning against a tree at the front of the house. This had happened several times and she wished the girl to be told to stay away from the property. He suggested that Selina would know more about the girl than he did, and Selina was summoned to discuss the ghost with her Ladyship. It eventually became accepted that Craycombe House was haunted. The late Viscount Cobham was kind enough to confirm this – when he lived at Craycombe as a small child, he remembered 'the girl in white' visiting his nursery, and he watched her walking through the nursery furniture. His sister described the orangery as 'pretty creepy'.

Chapter Four

Keeping the
Home Fires Burning

In the Chapel of Ease in Moor, there is stained glass by Francis Keat in the twin lancet windows at the east end of the church. It solemnly commemorates two worthy but very different women; Annie Elizabeth Gibbs 1865–1901 and Ellen Gibbs 1865–1933. They were the first and second wives of Walter Gibbs, who himself died in 1931.

Before the war cast its dark shadow, the Gibbs family had settled into to a more normal family life after its recent traumas. Walter Gibbs' beloved first wife, Annie Elizabeth, had died from breast cancer in 1901, leaving him with two-year-old daughter Alice and a premature baby son, Donald. His fragile son was despatched to his sister in Yorkshire, and Walter and Alice returned to live with his formidable mother in the family home, Vine Cottage in Moor.

Walter Gibbs was an established blacksmith and a well respected member of the local community. He was a member of Pershore Board of Guardians. He was People's Warden at Fladbury Church and a Church Land Trustee. He was a Manager at Fladbury School as well as a Moor Parish Councillor.

He was left several thousand pounds by his first wife, and became a man of some means. He had already built himself a large new blacksmith's shop, and proceeded to build around Vine Cottage, turning it into a large, detached Edwardian villa. At the same time, he bought more of the agricultural land that surrounded the house, which was renamed Bredon View. Walter planted his new orchard with 'Anne Elizabeth' apple trees. Local folk watched the building work with curiosity. They called the house 'Barley's Folly' – Barley being the maiden name of Annie Elizabeth, the love of Walter's life.

Alice's miserable early childhood at the mercy of Grandma Gibbs ended when her father married the gentle Ellen James, an old school friend of her mother's, in 1904. Ellen came from a local farming family. This event was followed swiftly by the death of Grandma Gibbs. Even the Moor villagers said, "Er was 'ard!" Nevertheless, Walter gave his mother the first 'black plumed horses and dray' funeral in Lower Moor.

Alice's early childhood left scars that would never fade. She continued to be shy and retiring for the rest of her life. She learned very early to watch and observe people and to adjust her behaviour accordingly. This tactic resulted in a more peaceful path. She had an enquiring mind and became a great lover of books.

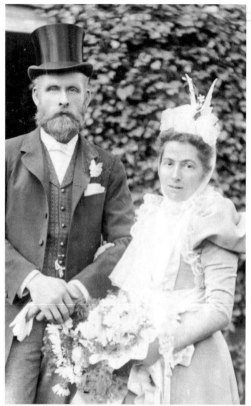

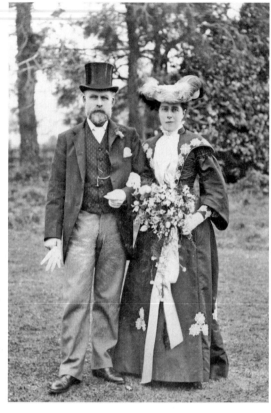

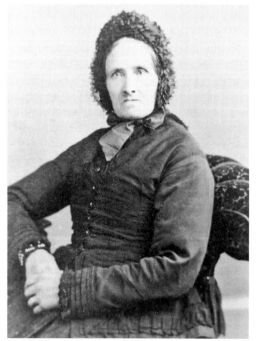

Above left: Walter and Annie Gibbs.

Above right: The wedding of Walter and Ellen Gibbs.

Left: 'Poor dear' Grandma Gibbs.

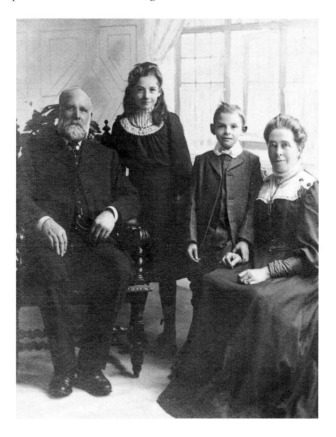

The reunited Gibbs family.

Her brother Donald returned from Yorkshire when he was four years old, completing the new Gibbs family. He left behind Ethel Bland and Louise Allatt, two adoring cousins, who had both helped to rear him.

There had been a Gibbs family in Moor since Oliver Cromwell's time and each generation had produced a village blacksmith.

Walter's life was a busy one; he dealt with the needs of six working farms as well as Springhill Farm. He employed another blacksmith, Fred Spiers, affectionately known as 'Clunk', who stayed with him for forty years. Fred Spiers was apt to greet customers with a gloomy 'How did you do this then?' usually adding, 'It'll take a bit of mendin'.'

There were always horses to be shod and Walter entered these into his account book under their own names: 'Blossom 4 shoes; Buttercup 4 shoes; Blackbird 4 shoes' – all with the date and the cost. There were a variety of jobs to do, like mending a wind instrument for Peopleton's village band or rising early to roughshod the milkman's horse on an icy morning. Many village boys were drawn to the Smithy to watch the blacksmiths at work. They filled their lungs with the steam from the hot iron and steel that was plunged into tubs of cold water for hardening.

The boys would watch the colour, red until it paled to a straw colour, run down the hot steel when it was being tempered. Then they would watch the blacksmith plunge the metal into the tub of cold water. They loved the ring of the anvils and the beat of the striker's hammers.

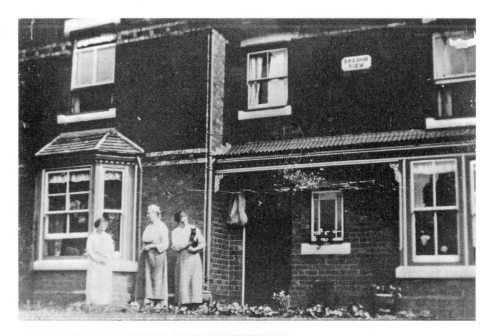

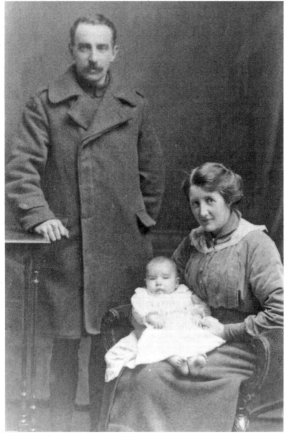

Above: Bredon View. Ellen Gibbs is in the centre, Alice is taking care of the cat.

Left: Harry and Louise Allatt with their son Anthony.

Village boys would volunteer to hold the horses or help blow the bellows. If they were lucky, they could buy an iron hoop for 1*d* and stop to see it made. They would watch as Walter selected a length of iron rod and shape it into a hoop. Then he would make a pot hook. He never seemed to burn his fingers on the black hot iron, like the boys sometimes did. They were always fascinated by the vast quantities of homemade cider that both blacksmiths consumed – yet neither of them appeared inebriated.

In winter, when the cold wind chilled people to the bone, little Jack Clark would seek out the warmth of the blacksmith's shop. Invariably, one of the men would find a piece of bread and cheese from their lunchbox for the small mite to eat.

Walter Gibbs was said by all who knew him to be 'one of nature's gentlemen', but he was not always so nice with his family. He was stern and highly critical of his daughter; expectations of his first-born were high. He recognised her intelligence when Henry Bancks, the Fladbury schoolmaster, pointed it out to him. Alice was sent to Prince Henry's Grammar School in Evesham. She was an accomplished pianist like her mother and a gifted needlewoman, but this cut no ice with Walter.

The newly married Ellen Gibbs was delighted with her stepson, Donald. His delicate waif-like looks tugged at her heartstrings and the pair got on well together from the start. Unlike Alice, Donald held no fond memories of his birth mother.

Alice was a dutiful daughter to Ellen and Walter and readily accepted Ellen's fondness for her only sister Polly's five children, Alice, Raymond, John, Annie, and Kathleen Wood. The family seemed happy once more, although years later, relatives who knew the new Mrs Gibbs as 'Aunt Ellen' would say that she and Walter shared a bed but 'nothing more'.

Ellen's sister Polly was seven years older, but they shared the same birthday. She married John Wood, a farmer's son from Pinvin, in 1885 when he was made a bailiff at Hill Court in Throckmorton for Benjamin Workman, a one-time Mayor of Evesham. When John died in 1908, Polly returned to their brother George at the family home, Norchard House in Peopleton, four miles or so from Lower Moor.

Alice had to inscribe five black-edged envelopes with 'In loving memory of dear Uncle John' before her father was satisfied that his ten-year-old daughter had done her best. Personally, Alice felt that Jesus was very welcome to her so-called Uncle John Wood. To add to her annoyance, Alice was asked by Ellen to give Kathleen Wood, John's youngest daughter, her favourite little clock to comfort her for the loss of her dear father. Alice was rewarded for her sacrifice with a 'trumpery little vase' from her stepmother Ellen, much to her displeasure.

Before her marriage, Annie Wood, Polly's second daughter, had trained with her younger sister Alice to work in the Refreshment Rooms, Reading for the Great Western Railway Company. They were trained to become future Refreshment Rooms manageresses in other parts of the company. The girls lived in a hostel above the Refreshment Rooms at Reading, under the watchful eye of their trainer, the housekeeper. They would often recall the hectic time they had in early August 1914 when the station tried to cope with a mass of troop trains. The two girls did well with the company and were promoted. Alice was sent to Tenby and Annie to Newport. It was during her training in Reading that Alice Wood met her future husband, Fred Hodges. Fred also worked for the Great Western until he joined the Army in 1915. Annie returned to Peopleton from Newport and married Tom Shenton in 1914.

Kathleen was the baby of the Wood family and a probationary nurse at a hospital in Leamington. Raymond Wood was Ellen's favourite nephew. He joined the Worcestershire

Regiment early in the war and served in France and Italy, eventually becoming a sergeant. His brother John joined the Army in 1918 and was swiftly despatched to Egypt. Alice Gibbs had no option but to make the best of the friendship the Wood girls provided, but she would shy away from their family celebrations whenever possible. Donald was a more sociable animal, much to Ellen's relief.

After her marriage to Walter, Ellen became closer to her delicate sister Polly and her five children. His working hours and 'public life' took up a great deal of his time, so personal time spent in companionship with her husband was sparse. Ellen's marriage to Walter at the age of thirty-nine saved her from a life spent in service to her own family. She was the daughter who stayed at home to help her mother. She would have become 'a woman of no importance', as many single women were destined to become in those times. These unfortunate single ladies were known as 'run arounds', for they were expected to help out, having not the ties of marriage and family. Ellen, as Walter's wife, had a certain amount of social standing in her extended family and in the parish, so she did not complain about her lot. She was a faithful correspondent to those of Walter's extended family who had moved away. Ellen enjoyed writing to her brother's daughter, Florrie, who had emigrated with her husband Archie and their son Bobbie to Vancouver Island, Canada.

Walter's nieces, Ethel Bland and Louise Allatt, had both played a large part in nurturing Donald as a delicate baby. They lived in Hooten Pagnell, South Yorkshire. Both of them had married men who before the war worked for Mrs Ward-Aldham on her South Yorkshire estate. After their mother's death, both Ethel and Louise kept up a regular correspondence with Ellen, as did Walter's youngest brother, Edwin, who lived with his wife and family in Malmsbury, Wiltshire. Ellen kept in touch with Walter's nephew Arthur and his wife Mary, who lived in Bridgenorth.

Ellen was an excellent housekeeper who kept a good table. She was a welcoming hostess to the extended family when they returned to Bredon View for family holidays. Secretly she rather enjoyed the change of company and the chance to laugh and gossip. It made a welcome change from the fraught atmosphere, when any form of illness threatened Walter. It was especially good to see Alice enjoying the family visits.

What follows is a snapshot of domestic life at Bredon View during the First World War.

Lighting: The downstairs rooms were lit with oil lamps called Belge Burners; upstairs it was candles only, making it very dark and eerie at night.

The privy: Going to the privy during the winter months was like preparing for an expedition to the North Pole. It was a mission not to be undertaken lightly. The privy was situated fifty yards up the garden from the kitchen door. In winter, they always took a candle lantern with them. Walter insisted that the children wear a warm coat and scarf, even a hat!

Bath time: Taking a bath was one of the weekly family manoeuvres and took place over the weekend. Outside the kitchen door were two water pumps; one for soft rainwater and the other for hard water. Soft water was pumped into buckets and heated up in the kitchen copper on the coal-fired kitchen range. It was then hauled upstairs to the small box room they called 'the dressing room', where the tin bath resided. Donald

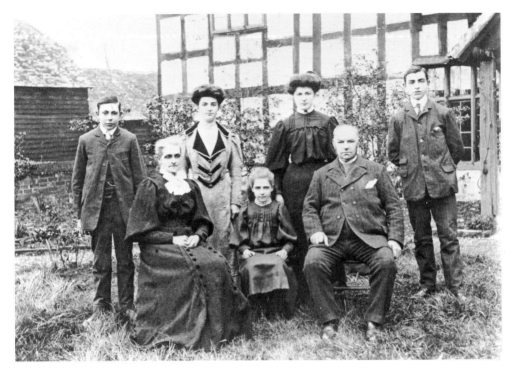

The Wood family (from left to right): John, Polly, Annie, Kathleen, Alice, John, Raymond.

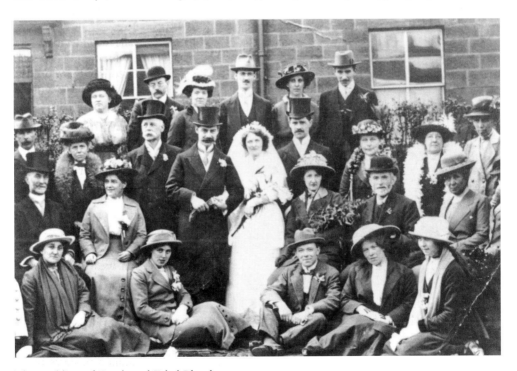

The wedding of Frank and Ethel Bland.

was the first to take a bath before he left for Peopleton on Saturday morning. Next came Ellen, who took her bath on Saturday afternoon, then Alice bathed on Saturday evening. Finally it was Walter, who took his bath before he left for church on Sunday morning. Getting rid of the used bath water was a chore, as it meant many journeys up and down the stairs carrying the used soapy water. There was a small window in the box room and Donald occasionally attempted to empty buckets of the bath water out of the window, down a small bay and on to the path below. This, however, engaged the wrath of his stepmother, for the soapy fluid wreaked havoc with her prize geraniums in the flowerbeds below.

Bedtime: Alice was well into her teens before she took supper at 9.00 p.m. with her parents and was allowed to stay up until ten. Before that, it was always bed at 8.00 p.m., although she was allowed to read for a little while by the light of the candle – though she had to blow it out as soon as she heard Walter and Ellen retire for the night. When they came to visit, her teenage town cousins were horrified by such early bedtimes – although they were usually exhausted by the amount of walking that was expected of them on a visit to Bredon View, so an early night was welcome. It appeared to them that to do anything entertaining or of any interest required many miles of walking.

Chapter Five

The Gibbs in 1918

Adapted from the 1918 diary of Ellen Gibbs of Bredon View, Lower Moor near Pershore, Worcestershire.

Donald Gibbs' present to his stepmother Ellen at Christmas 1917 was a large diary from Boots. She promised him that she would write in it every day.

Tuesday 1 January 1918 had drizzling rain first thing in the morning and was cold and dull for the rest of the day. Ellen managed to finish the washing and Walter spent the day 'clerking' (doing his accounts), which she encouraged him to do, for it was a job that irritated him – he tended to put the evil off at the slightest excuse. Charles Firs, the Belgian refugee from Fladbury, sent a card of good wishes through the post. Walter went into Pershore and on his way back he called in at The Croft in Moor to see his brother George, who was far from well. Miss Willis Bund from the Old Manor House called with her tall lanky niece Penelope to wish them all a Happy New Year.

The following day started with a sharp frost, followed by a fine, clear day. Papers about voluntary rationing were brought to the house, inviting the Gibbs household to join the National Food Economy League.

The papers suggested that for men like Walter, engaged in very heavy work, 8 lb of bread was recommended for consumption a week. Men on sedentary work were reduced to 5 lb of bread a week. Women doing heavy or agricultural work were also advised to consume 5 lb of bread. Women in ordinary industrial or domestic service were to be allowed 4 lb of bread. Women unoccupied (a term which amused Ellen) or on sedentary work were allowed 3 lb 8 oz of bread. The 'war bread' was beginning to look a dirty grey colour because a larger and larger percentage of flour was being extracted.

In addition, people were to be allowed the following weekly ration: 2 lb of meat for each person; 12 oz of cereals; 10 oz of butter, margarine, lard, and other fats; and 8 oz of sugar.

Ellen digested the facts sent by Lord Devonport, a one-time provision merchant who was in charge of the new Ministry of Food. While she did so, she settled down by the fire in the sitting room to make two tablecloths for everyday use while Alice embroidered the regimental badge of the Worcestershire Regiment on to a table centre for her Aunt Polly.

Raymond, Polly's eldest son and Ellen's favourite nephew, was with the Worcesters in Italy. Raymond, along with several other local boys, had been sent from France to Italy in 1917.

The following day, Ellen received a letter from Polly enclosing four of Raymond's letters, the last one dated Christmas Eve. She sadly recorded that Sidney Hunt, son of William Hunt, had died of his wounds in France on the 26 December. His parents had received official notification that very morning, a week after his death.

Ellen looked in the *Evesham Journal* to see that James Bomford of Springhill had been awarded the Military Cross after the battle of Cambria in France. She also noticed that the price of the *Journal* had been raised ½d; it was now 2d a copy!

Sunday 6 January was the Day of National Supplication and Thanksgiving in churches across the country. It began with Holy Communion at 8.00 a.m. Rector Lawson took the service at Fladbury in the morning and the evening and the offertory for the Red Cross was £9 19s. Ellen thought it most suitable; the casualty list seemed to grow each time she read the *Parish Magazine*.

Ernest Payne was in a Glasgow hospital suffering from shell shock and Oliver Woolloff's death was the third death in his family. Ellen remembered Oliver working for the Smyth family at the Manor House in Fladbury in happier times, before this terrible war started.

Noted in the *Parish Magazine* was the news that Sir Charles Swinfen Eady, Master of the Rolls, who now owned the Wood Norton Estate, had sent £4 to be distributed to some of the poor in the parish.

Ellen decided to write to her nephew Raymond, who was still somewhere in Italy.

The following day, Ellen woke to a white world. There had been quite a sprinkling of snow, which froze as the day went on. It was so cold the following morning that their washing water was frozen in the water jug in their bedroom.

That day, Ellen realised that the condition of Walter's brother George, the one-time village shoemaker, was very serious. When Ellen and Walter visited him he just lay there taking no notice of anyone.

Mrs Adams of Craycombe Farm had called in at the blacksmith's shop and told Walter that her daughter, Edith Eleanor, better known as Dolly, was to be married to Albert Spencer on 19 January. This was a surprise for everyone. Ellen considered the fun-loving Dolly a shade flighty and was most surprised to learn that she had consented to settle down to married life. Mrs Adams was related by marriage to Polly, Ellen's sister. Craycombe farm belonged to Craycombe House, once the Dower House on the Duc d'Orléans' estate at nearby Fladbury.

Thursday 10 January was Raymond Wood's birthday. His last one was spent in France; this one was in Italy. Perhaps next year's would be spent at home, wrote Ellen.

Ellen and Alice took a trip on the train into Evesham in search of a winter coat. They finished up at Hamilton and Bells, where they bought a coat for Alice.

On Saturday 12 January, George Gibbs died. He was sixty-five years old. His son Isaac came to Bredon View to tell them. Ellen went down to the house of mourning straight away to help Mrs Cole with the laying out. She thought George looked very peaceful and noted that it was a happy change for him. Walter wrote to the rest of the family to notify them of George's death.

Ellen missed going to church that Sunday because her niece Annie Shenton called on her way to Craycombe Farm for dinner with her husband Thomas. The ill-assorted couple were married in Peopleton early in 1914 and Alice Gibbs had been one of their bridesmaids. They had requested as one of their wedding hymns 'Fight the Good Fight', and as far as Ellen was concerned they had never stopped.

Ellen's nieces and nephews, Alice, Annie, and John, lived locally and were always calling in at Bredon View to see her, probably because she made them so welcome.

On Monday 14 January, the weather remained troublesome. Snow continued to fall and it was very cold. The roads were in a dreadful state.

On Tuesday morning, Ellen trudged down to The Croft at about 4.00 p.m. to help Mrs Cole put poor George into his coffin. They had a letter the following morning from Walter's sister Louise and her husband John Arlidge, caretakers at Old Scotland Yard in London, to say that they would not be coming to George's funeral. But they did send a cheque to help with expenses.

On Wednesday 16 January, the day of George's funeral, the snow was eight inches deep in places, covering Ellen's shoe tops as she walked down to The Croft to help Mrs Cole put 'the finishing touches to poor George'.

The church at Moor was a Chapel of Ease, built so that the aged and infirm of the village could attend a church regularly. It was not licensed for weddings or funerals so these ceremonies were held at the Church of Saint John the Baptist in Fladbury.

Funerals were great occasions for all concerned. Certain norms prevailed in the small community and observance was sometimes rigid. The coffin, made by the village carpenter, Jim Hundy, was always delivered at night. Lying in their beds, folk could hear the 'tramp, tramp, tramp' along the lane – this sound told them that the coffin was being carried to the house of mourning. Homemade wreaths and posies were always taken after tea time, for it was considered a more discreet time to call. Most folk called with flowers and were expected to view the body. Some ladies were laid to rest in their wedding nightgown. All the bodies wore long white stockings.

On the day of the funeral, the villagers of Moor closed their curtains as a mark of respect when the funeral procession passed by on its way to the church, which was two miles away. The funeral progressed out of the village and along Porters Path, crossing the railway at the level crossing and taking the footpath leading to Coach Drive. Finally, the procession would join Station Road to reach the church in Fladbury.

The 'walking funeral' at Fladbury Church was at 2.30 p.m., but as the roads and paths along Porters Path were so snow-ridden, George's widow Gertie and Ellen could not attend. Only Walter and Isaac, George's son, followed the coffin. It was placed upon a bier with rubber wheels that was pushed two miles by four of the village men. In Moor, Thomas Oldham from Manor Farm and Mr Yates were 'falling in' as the funeral passed by their houses.

Until 1900, the deceased were carried in their coffin by six male bearers. Every bearer was presented with a pair of black kid gloves especially for the occasion. It was not until 1900 that moor owned a bier on rubber wheels. The money for the bier was raised at a village fête during the summer of 1900.

A great deal more snow fell during the night and in the morning the trees were laden. Ellen's niece Alice Wood called in. She was going to stay with her aunt at Craycombe Farm. Her cousin Dolly was to be married on Saturday and there was a great deal to do.

She left a letter with Ellen from her mother and one from her brother Raymond, describing his Christmas Day in Italy. He said that they had a nice little service in the open air on Christmas morning. All around the Italian countryside the bells were ringing. It sounded quite beautiful and reminded him of England. They had Christmas dinner at 4.30 p.m. – roast pork, cabbage, and potatoes, followed by plum pudding. After dinner, everyone had an apple, cigarettes, chocolates, and wine. They did not

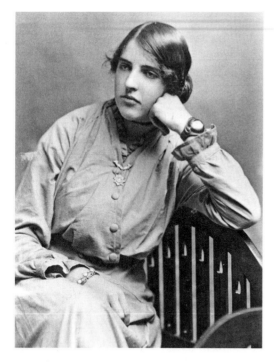

Kathleen Wood.

have a table or plates but sat on the floor and ate out of their mess tins and thoroughly enjoyed it. They were billeted in a village well behind the lines, where they could have a rest from the fighting.

At home a rapid thaw had set in. The lane outside Bredon View was like a brook, but by evening the water had subsided. Young Percy Cotterill, a friend of Donald's, called in to tell them that Polly's daughter Kathleen was very ill in Leamington Hospital, where she was nursing. Her temperature was 101 degrees Fahrenheit.

The following Saturday, 19 January, Edith Eleanor (Dolly) Adams was married to Albert Victor Spencer at Fladbury Church. Dolly had been active in the parish, organising whist drives and entertainments for her friends' and neighbours' pleasure and to benefit good causes, so she had many well wishers at her wedding. Ellen Gibbs didn't have much to say about the marriage except, 'No sunshine for that wedding'.

Ellen was more than glad to see the oilman, as the night before they the oil lamps had gone out and they'd had to light candles. Ellen noted that paraffin was now two shillings a gallon.

Miss Lawson, the Rector's daughter, came to ask Donald to sell tickets for 'the Entertainment' on Thursday at the Parish Room in Fladbury. Five ladies and three gentlemen from 'The Pershore Magpies' were visiting. Ellen paid her annual subscription of five shillings to the District Nursing Fund, which covered the wages of their District Nurse, based in Fladbury. Donald spent the afternoon tramping around Hill Furze, Wyre, and Throckmorton, delivering bills for his father.

On 22 January, Ellen noticed the first snowdrops peeping up in the garden. Mrs Janet Bomford of Springhill called in the afternoon to ask Walter for a subscription to the Moor Clothing Club.

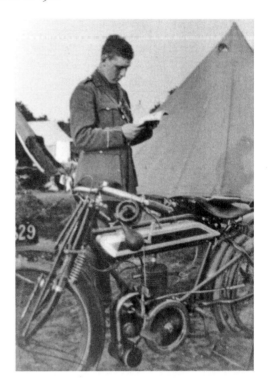

James Bomford.

The Club provided money for the parish poor to buy clothes. Her son James was now Captain Bomford, MC. She was so proud, noted Ellen.

The Gibbs received a letter from Edwin, Walter's younger brother in Malmsbury. He told of the difficulties they had obtaining provisions. They could get little milk, butter, cheese, or meat. On Monday 27 January, Ellen despatched a small parcel to Edwin and his young family containing a piece of pig meat, lard, and a few apples. A similar parcel was sent to another of Walter's relatives, Ethel Bland, who lived in Hooten Pagnell, South Yorkshire.

They received an interesting letter from Ethel's husband Frank Bland, from 'somewhere in France'. He was no longer a signaller and had been transferred to the Royal Engineers. He was not able to say what his work was but said that it was interesting and not too hard, about a mile behind the firing line. He and another fellow, a London-Irish chap called Patsy, lived in a little hut about six feet square and seven feet high, boarded all round with a corrugated iron roof with earth piled on top of it. They had a table and a chair and a stove brought from a nearby village. They did their own cooking when on duty. Frank had about three miles to walk to work and said it was so sad to see the devastation and desolation for miles around. The ground that was once flat was a mass of huge shell holes joined together like a huge black macabre necklace. Walter thought that Frank was probably laying mines.

Walter's dreaded gout flared up so he had taken to his bed. Alice cycled to Pershore to fetch him some medication from the chemist. The following day, Walter was well enough to read and enjoy Alice's Christmas present to him, *Pearl of Pearl Island*.

The next day, Walter was much better, and he arose from his bed after dinner.

The Rector called to say that he had engaged a curate, a Reverend Blower, who had married two months ago to a widow with a little girl aged about eight. They were coming to live at St Catherine's along the lane from Bredon View.

Alice was busy with her needlecraft and had finished working the regimental badges for her Yorkshire cousins, Louise Allatt and Ethel Bland. Harry Allatt's badge for the Flying Corps looked very pretty and dainty on a pincushion and Frank Bland's badge of the Yorkshire and Lancashire Regiment was very handsome on a cushion cover. She had packed them up ready to send tomorrow.

They had news of Kathleen Wood that day. Polly had heard from the matron at Leamington Hospital, who said that Kathleen was suffering from 'sub-acute rheumatism'. She was somewhat better and able to sit up and take a little 'Bengers Food'.

On the last day of January, Ellen received letters from Ethel Bland and Edwin Gibbs. They were both delighted with the content of their parcels. Ethel wrote from Yorkshire to say that so far they had not had to eat dry bread as they had got some jam which they had made before sugar got so scarce. But for three weeks they could not get butter, bacon, lard, or margarine, and they had very little meat, so the present was doubly welcome.

On 1 February 1918, Walter planted two plum trees given by the Rector to Donald and Alice. Walter had not heeded Sir Walter Scott's gardener's words, 'Plant a tree before Candlemas, you may command it to grow, after Candlemas you may beg it to grow.' Only time would tell.

On Monday 4 February, Walter and Donald went to the Evesham Candlemas Fair and took time off to buy Donald a suit that cost £1 15s 6d. Ellen stayed at home and wrote a long letter to her niece Florrie, who was living a hard life with her husband Archibald Lewis and her son Bobbie on Vancouver Island. Ellen sent her the *Evesham Journal* so she could keep up to date with things at home. Florrie longed to come home to see her father and her two aunts.

That evening, a maid from the Rectory and two Fladbury girls came over to ask for a subscription for prizes and cakes for the whist drive on Shrove Tuesday, in aid of the Parochial Fund. They were given 5s.

On 7 February, Rector Lawson called in the afternoon to leave a 'Roll of Honour for the Dead' card to be placed on Moor's church door. Mrs Francis of The Brooklands, Fladbury, who had lost her son in the war, had volunteered them for all the church doors in the parish. There were thirteen names for Fladbury and seven for the hamlet of Moor. Throckmorton had two names and Wyre had one. Many families who had been bereaved wanted the names of their dead commemorated with a memorial in church and this 'Roll of Honour' brought fleeting comfort to those who had lost a young life.

The tablet in Moor's church bore the following names that had given their lives for the sake of freedom, 1914-18:

Charles J. Cole
A. Ernest Collins
Arthur W. Phillips
Harvey Pratt
Arthur H. Sheward
Harold B. Sheward
A. Bernard Sorrell
Walter F. Wooten

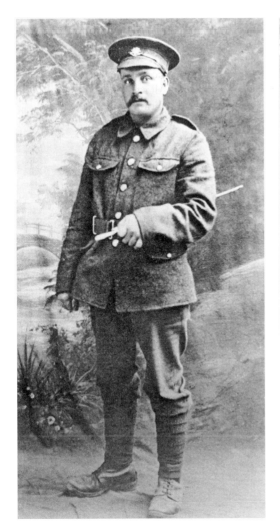 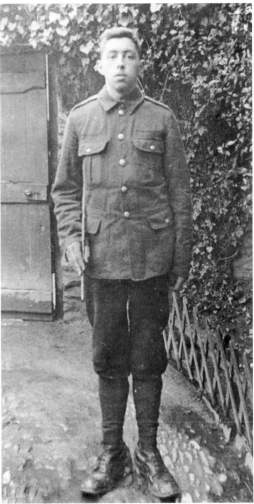

Charles J. Cole (left) and Harold B. Sheward (right). Both of these Moor boys died for their country. Their families are still in the village.

Ellen was bewildered by the shadow of death all round her and the terrible loss of precious young lives. She worried about her nephew and other young relatives who were serving their country. She was shocked to see many local boys come home traumatised, both physically and mentally. You could see the haunted look in their eyes as some of them returned home on leave.

Many, for the sake of their nearest and dearest, assumed a normality that they did not feel. The men could talk to one another but few talked to their families for once they had unburdened themselves to their nearest and dearest and returned to active service, their families lived in greater fear than before. Sometimes Ellen was allowed to read some of the censored letters sent home to anxious mothers; she found the letters painful to read.

A brother with the British Expeditionary Force in France writes to his sister:

Dear Sister,

Just a few lines to let you know I am quite well and hope that you are the same.

I do not write often but it is not because I don't think of you all at home, perhaps you are often disappointed and I am very sorry. I like to receive your letters and I always get a letter from home before the parcel comes soon afterwards. I am very glad to know that the cigarettes are coming, we don't get many cigarettes here, in fact not enough and you must please thank Father for the weekly lot that he sends. Please let me know how my brother and sisters are in your next letter, with love to Mother and Father.

A last letter from a son on the Somme, dated 15 November 1916:

Dear Mother,

It is some time since I last wrote and I hope that you have not been worrying, for I am quite all right though there is not much to write about. I thought that I would just let you know that I am safe. I thank you very much for the money you sent, it is most useful when coming out of the trenches and I have the pleasure of a few extras to meals by buying a few things that we cannot usually get. I have not told you before that I am on the Sniping section that is proving an interesting business. I have been on it about a month now. The officer who called upon you at our house is my commanding officer. Cousin Andrew wishes to be remembered to you all and now I must close with fondest love to you all, your loving son, George.

This was the last letter the young soldier wrote for he was reported missing believed killed the very next day.

Ellen felt that she could say nothing and do nothing to relieve the agony of grief that the mothers were going through, apart from take a posy of flowers or a few eggs to the house of mourning. Ellen did what she knew best, and that was to lead a busy life. She even made a daily note as to how many eggs their six hens laid.

Despite the gloom there was a light-hearted note when Alice told her of the white wedding held at Pershore Abbey on 9 February when Dr Asham and Miss Machin of Stanhope House, Pershore were married. Alice described the four bridesmaids, who were dressed in white, and the pageboy, who wore a white sailor suit.

Of course, the happy couple had the usual white slipper attached to their car when going away and some wag had left, on the back window of their car, a big card with the words 'Newly Wed' in large letters, which caused much amusement.

Ellen found time to send a box of snowdrops to her niece, Kathleen, still in hospital in Leamington. The poor girl had to be in bed for several weeks, because her pains had returned.

One Friday afternoon in the middle of February, Ellen walked with Mrs Workman from Holly House in Moor to the weekly War Working Party, held at the Manor House in Fladbury. Nearby, Chadbury House was to be used as a Red Cross hospital. It would be an annexe to nearby Abbey Manor Hospital. Mrs Haines Rudge of Abbey Manor had appealed, through Mrs Janet Bomford and Mrs Elizabeth Smyth, for funds. Mrs Elizabeth Smyth suggested to the War Working Party that they take a special interest in one of the ten-bedded wards.

Ellen had her first visit from new curate Reverend Blower, and found him a plain but pleasant man. The following day, Walter went into Worcester on the train to pay a bill. He could not get anything in the way of 'eatables' to bring home. A shop with 'Horse Flesh for Sale' had opened in Lowersmoor, a suburb of the city. He said a good many people were looking at the meat, but he did not see anyone go in to make a purchase. People were now only allowed about 8oz of butcher's meat per head per week. That week, Mr Tolley, the Fladbury butcher, sent them 2lb 5oz of beef, which cost 1s 5d per pound.

On 21 February, after several days of bright spring sunshine, Ellen's thoughts turned to spring-cleaning. Alice had her half-day from Mrs Tillman's dressmaking establishment in Pershore on a Thursday, so Ellen and Alice tackled the cleaning of the household brasses.

The crocuses made a lovely splash of colour in the front garden border and Ellen covered up another root of rhubarb under the zinc bath. (Shutting out light and holding the heat is a technique for quickening rhubarb growth, known in some quarters as the 'Yorkshire forced' technique.)

Sad news arrived the following day, when Polly sent a long letter from Peopleton with the baker's boy. News had been received of William Loxley, who had died of wounds at a base hospital in France. Poor William – Ellen had known him as a boy and liked him.

On Saturday 23 February, they received a photograph of Mary Gibbs and the new baby, Grace Mary. They were the wife and daughter of Arthur, Walter's nephew, who lived near Bridgenorth. They all agreed that the new baby looked 'a regular little Arthur'.

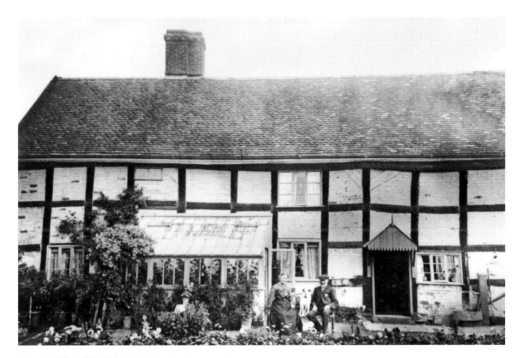

Mr and Mrs Workman at Holly House, Moor.

When he was young, Arthur's father, Alfred, decided to have a career in service. He joined Rector Haviland's household in Fladbury to become a valet. All went well until love blossomed between Alfred and Mrs Haviland's lady's maid, Elizabeth Brown. It caused a great drama in 1864 when the couple eloped to London. The autocratic Mrs Haviland arrived at Vine Cottage in Moor and swept up the front path to confront his parents, Harriet and Isaac Gibbs. 'She's run off to marry your beardless boy!' she angrily declared. His brother Walter was despatched to London to bring back the hapless married couple. Alfred's chosen career was over and he moved away from home to work at Billingsley Colliery, Staffordshire, where he eventually became the manager.

Unfortunately, Walter's gout threatened to rear its ugly head again and he was confined to bed after a bad night with his foot. Ellen got some hot water with soda and salt and bathed it before she accompanied Alice to the 8.00 a.m. communion service in Moor.

After breakfast, Donald went to Pershore to fetch his father some medicine. Walter's foot was a little better, but he'd had another night of pain. Ellen bathed his foot again before breakfast. With any spare time that she could steal away from the invalid, Ellen spent gathering enough flower and herb roots to fill a nice large box to post to Louise Arlidge, Walter's sister, for their new garden in Wallington near London.

The following day was a busy one for Ellen. Fortunately, Walter had a better night. She was up very early to prepare for the visit of the diminutive sweep from Pershore, Mr Daniels, timed for 7.00 a.m. He would arrive on his bike and get on with his task, trying not to create too much mess. Ellen had a love-hate relationship with this fellow, for he always tried to take the soot away for his own garden if he was not challenged. 'His Lordship' – as she called him – arrived at 10.00 a.m., much to Ellen's displeasure. It was late when she had cleared up and could light the fire.

They had a welcome letter from Edwin, Walter's brother in Malmsbury, to say that he had got the post of School Attendance Officer for North West Wiltshire. Walter and Ellen were very pleased and felt the position would benefit him considerably, although the work would only involve four days a week.

Walter, thank goodness, was better, and he decided to get up for tea. He had managed to read three books while he was laid up in bed: *The Devil's Disciple* by William de Quincy, *The Scapegoat* by Hall Caine, and *The Mistress of Shinston* by Mrs Barclay.

In the evening, Donald went to an 'entertainment' in Fladbury, performed by some players from leading London theatres in aid of the Red Cross. He came home full of what he had seen, but added that he would have preferred a concert by local people. What taste! Ellen sometimes despaired of him.

March came in like a lion and Ellen had to struggle along the mile-long Porters Path to Mrs Smyth's War Working Party, where she heard that Mrs David Clark of The Buildings, Coach Drive had contracted scarlet fever and had been taken to the sanatorium. The Buildings were far from perfect dwellings, as they were converted cowsheds used by the Bomfords to house the hop-pickers from Dudley, who arrived at Springhill every year.

On 2 March, Donald was seventeen years old. He went into Evesham for his copy of *The Boy's Own Paper* and did several errands for Ellen. She was pleased with the two half-pint cups he bought for four pennies each. Walter worked in the forge but was not feeling first class. His sister Louise wrote to thank Ellen for the plants that she had sent them.

Early in March, one of the men who worked for Walter brought in five strong, healthy chickens. They were put into a pen on the grass to protect them from Snip the dog, who was very keen to chase them. Walter, Donald, and Fred Spires were digging in the garden during all the time they could spare from the blacksmith's shop, to prepare the ground for planting.

Ellen's niece Annie called in and told Ellen that an aeroplane had landed in Pinvin and was lying in the field by their house. She thought Donald might like to pop over to see it in the morning. The following day, Donald went over to Pinvin to see the plane before it sped on its way at about 10.00 a.m. – after having a little circular flight and looping the loop for the benefit of the small crowd that had gathered in the field.

Sunday 10 March was, as usual, busy with churchgoing. It occupied most people in the parish. Fladbury Church held two services on a Sunday. The morning service was attended by what Ellen called 'top terrace people', who had servants at home preparing their Sunday lunch. Middle terrace folk – ordinary mortals – had to stay at home and tend the cooking on an open fire with the meat in the side oven. They attended church in the evening, when their main cooking chores were over.

On this Sunday, Ellen attended church in the morning. She heard that Josh Stephens from Fladbury Mill was wounded with a smashed wrist in France.

Walter went to Fladbury in the morning and Alice and Donald went to Fladbury in the evening. The Reverend Langley Frost, who spoke on behalf of the mission to the Jews in East London, took both services.

The following day, Walter was very unwell, his liver 'out of sorts'. He was dosing himself with pills and salts to help 'work it off'. The fact that his Normanton cooking apples had only made thirty shillings a pot at market in Pershore did not improve his mood. Later that day, however, he felt well enough to send another ten pots of apples to market and was paid thirty-two shillings per pot, the best price ever.

Walter went over to Mr Tolley, the butcher at Fladbury who had bought a small pig from him, to get the pig weighed. It weighed six score eleven pounds, for which Mr Tolley paid him twenty-five shillings per score. Not bad for a day's takings.

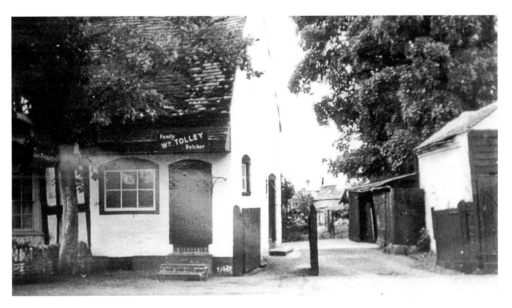

Mr Tolley's butcher's shop, Fladbury.

On Thursday 14 March, the spring-cleaning started in earnest. It was Alice's half-day Ellen and Alice tackled Donald's bedroom, where they took down the spare bedstead. Just as things were in full swing, Mr and Mrs Webb arrived from Fladbury. Ellen had to leave Alice and entertain them while their horse was shod. The same morning, Ellen had a letter from her sister Polly to say that she and Mrs Boucher, her neighbour, were obliged to have two lady hay-balers billeted with them. She was very upset, especially with her daughter Alice's wedding to Fred Hodges, which was imminent.

On Friday 15 March, when Ellen walked along Porters Path on her way to Mrs Smyth's War Working Party, she had to battle against a bitter north-easterly wind.

Mrs Smyth took a great interest in Alice's musical progress and often sent her gifts of sheet music. Mrs Smyth liked the gentle Ellen and would sometimes confide in her about her sister Mary, who was the widow of Adolf Holst. Mary had been a music student when she had met Adolf in Cheltenham.

For a while during the war, Mrs Holst had taken rooms with Clara Oldham at Manor Farm House in Moor. It appeared that Adolf Holst had not left his widow comfortably off. All the money had gone to furthering his son's musical career. Both Gustav and his wife were engaged in war work and Mary Holst led a lonely existence. Her sisters did what they could, but she caused them a great deal of anxiety.

The following Saturday, Mr Boulter, the Peopleton baker, brought her sister Polly over to stay. Ellen pulled her first rhubarb from the garden to bake into a tart.

Polly rested on Sunday and she and Ellen did a great deal of talking before Mr Boucher called for her at 5.30 p.m. to take her home. Walter and Ellen attended evensong at Fladbury Church. Rector Lawson took the service that commenced at 6.30 p.m. Ellen wrote with great indignation, 'We did not arrive home until 9pm after a very long and very tiresome sermon!'

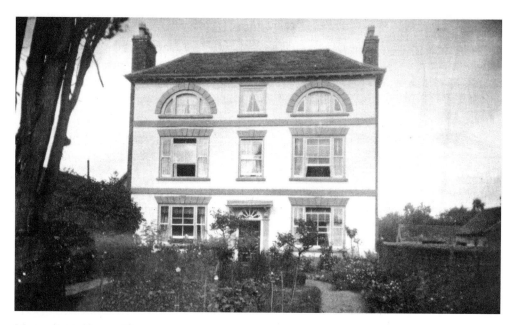

Manor Farm House, Moor.

Ellen had a letter from Louise Allatt, to say that husband Harry had been home on leave, so there had been great excitement. Louise thought he looked well. Harry had gone back the day she wrote her letter, so Ellen knew that it would imminently be a case of 'Poor Louise'.

To lighten the mood a little, she wrote in her diary that Polly had been to Pershore to be fitted for her dress for her daughter Alice's forthcoming wedding.

The following day, Ellen noted, was the birthday of Clara, the long-suffering wife of Thomas Oldham of Manor Farm House. Donald had taken her a posy of herbs and flowers as a gift from them all.

Thomas Oldham was one of Moor's most colourful characters. He was a former Regimental Sergeant-Major of the Royal Artillery and had campaign medals from Africa, China, Burma, and South Africa to prove it. He met Clara while visiting relations in Fladbury. Until then, Clara Eliza Stephens had lived with her family at Fladbury Mill. She was no longer young and was nearly past her prime. She viewed Thomas Oldham – who was tall, with a domed, bald head and tattooed arms – as perhaps her last chance of matrimony.

Their courtship was not smooth. Her brothers, George and Arthur, were not happy to see the inebriated Thomas coming to woo their sister. Clara became so used to this that she had a rowing boat ready for her tipsy suitor and she would row him up and down the river until he was sober enough to exchange polite talk with her family. This ploy did not fool her brothers, who were heard to mutter, "Er should 'ave drowned 'im'.

Thomas vowed to settle down and he married Clara. He rented Manor Farm in Moor. Unfortunately, he was not born to follow the plough. The Moor men scorned his poor farming methods. Folk said that you could see straight through his cows. His ploughed fields were known as 'Tommy's play tracts' and even his pigs were thought inferior.

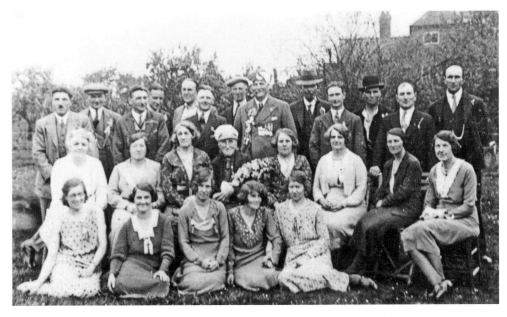

Thomas Oldham with his medals. Wife Clara is seated below him with a bouquet.

Clara struggled to manage the farm as best she could with the help of Berthe, a refugee from Belgium, while Thomas pursued worthy causes, using a three-wheel bicycle to transport himself around the parish. He was the life and soul of any party. He would sport a red, white, and blue tie with a red buttonhole and sing, with great gusto and at the drop of a hat, 'I'm a fine old English Gentleman'. It was suspected that he had a lady friend in Hill, a hamlet near Moor. There was a real giveaway, for everyone could see his three-wheel bicycle parked outside her house for fairly long periods of time.

On 20 March, there was great excitement when Mr Boulter drove Alice Wood over to say that Fred, her fiancé, had arrived home in Reading on leave. They wanted to arrange the wedding for Saturday at Fladbury Church. Alice went over to see the Rector and Mrs Bancks. The schoolmistress was to provide the small wedding reception at the schoolhouse.

The next day, Walter took Alice Wood into Worcester to get the marriage license. Alice bought herself a lovely biscuit-coloured wedding hat with an under brim of pale blue.

On 22 March, it was Ellen's turn to buy wedding finery and she took herself into Evesham to Tipper's Shop to get herself a wedding hat for *9s 6d* and a pair of grey gloves for *1s 11d*. When she got back home, the bridegroom Fred Hodges had already arrived to stay at Bredon View the night before his wedding.

He amused everyone when he said that he and Alice could not get married in the morning because the horses, needed to draw their bridal carriage, were to be put to the plough in the morning.

The wedding day, Saturday 23 March, was a lovely day of warm sunshine. A good omen for the happy pair, thought Ellen. The bride arrived at 2.00 p.m. at Fladbury Church wearing a white embroidered voile dress and her new hat. Fred's two sisters arrived on the train from Reading to act as bridesmaids. Unfortunately, they were both

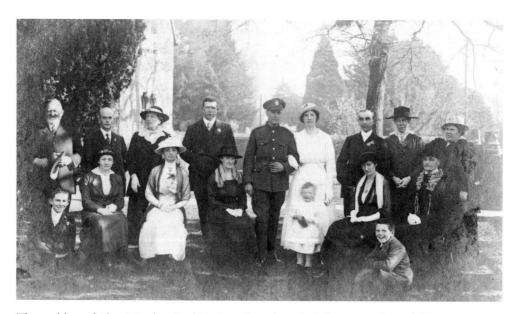

The wedding of Alice Wood to Fred Hodges. Seated on the left are Donald and Alice Gibbs. Ellen Gibbs is standing second from the right.

dressed in deep black and not in pink, the colour Alice had suggested. They insisted that they were still in mourning for their mother, so black was the colour they wore.

Alice's brother John gave her away and her cousin, Will James, was the best man. Mr Bancks played 'The Wedding March' and they sang hymn number 350, 'The Voice that Breathed o'er Eden', and hymn number 351, 'How Welcome Was the Call'.

The wedding reception afterwards was held at the schoolhouse for a few close friends of the bride and bridegroom.

Despite the excitement, Walter did not forget to put the clocks forward an hour that night ready for British Summer Time.

The following day was Palm Sunday, but Walter did not venture out as he had a warning of the return of his gout – probably from all the 'hard play' yesterday, wrote Ellen.

On Monday, he took to his bed for the day. Ellen heard from her niece Kathleen in Leamington that progress was very slow. There was some talk of her being taken out in the hospital grounds in a bath chair – which she would not enjoy, Ellen thought. The newlyweds were going to visit her that day for dinner.

On Wednesday 27 March it was cold and dull. At about 11.00 a.m., a Staff Sergeant called to ask the Gibbs to put up a couple of hay-balers. Walter, now recovered, tried to get out of it but Ellen felt the Sergeant pressed them somewhat and they really had no choice but to consent.

Ellen was promised 1s 3d a night, and the men would pay her for doing their cooking. They would also pay for milk and any vegetables. He did promise to send them tidy men. Lo and behold, the men arrived at 5.30 p.m. bringing with them their rations, bread, meat, margarine, tea, sugar, jam, and marmalade. After weighing them up for a couple of days, Ellen concluded that Edgar and Ben seemed satisfactory in every way. One was from London and the other was from Ilfracombe in Devon. They had both been invalided out of the fighting Army but were directed to work on the land.

Walter was over his gout but was far from well, suffering from severe indigestion. He had been in all day, reading and writing. Ellen and Alice both suspected that Walter was a hypochondriac, but it was more than their lives were worth to say so. His mood for the day depended upon how he felt when he opened his eyes in the morning. He was not an easy man to live with and was especially severe with his children, who tended to live in his shadow. Walter Gibbs was inclined to be a street angel but a home devil, which was covered up beautifully by the family.

When he was confined to bed, Walter had many visitors, but he was far from gracious about some of them. Miss Willis Bund called to bring him some fresh sea kale from her garden. His reply when Ellen told him was not Christian. 'Old maids can't grow vegetables!'

His least comforting visitor was her brother, the eminent Mr Willis Bund, KC. As Ellen was showing this grand gentleman out, she murmured to him about the difficulty of keeping her husband in his bed. The gentleman revolved on the doorstep and roared up the stairs, 'You stay where you are, Mrs Gibbs, take away his trousers!'

Good Friday fell on the 29 March. Strangely enough, this day was not spent as a quiet, holy day. Alice, who had the day off, gave the sitting room a thorough clean.

Ellen went over to Fladbury Church in the morning for part of the special three-hour service. She took some flowers for the Gibbs family graves. In the evening, she attended Moor Church for the service at 6.30 p.m. The people of the parish were very

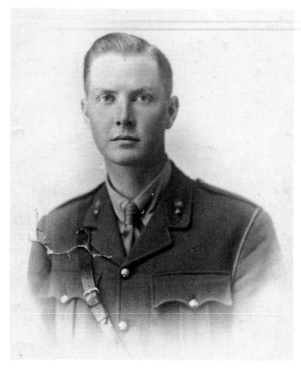

Harold Gibbs.

aware of the great battle being raged in France. It was the beginning of the Second Battle of the Somme.

The British Army were sending many inexperienced youths to France; even much older men were no longer considered safe from conscription.

On Easter Saturday, Walter and Ellen were told that Harold Gibbs, their nephew, had been killed the previous Monday in France. The poor lad had been writing to his parents at 9.00 a.m. At 3.00 p.m., he was seriously wounded in the chest, back, and legs by a German sniper. He died an hour after being taken to hospital. He was buried in a military cemetery. The grieving parents hoped to visit his grave when the terrible war was over. The whole family were very upset and Walter wrote immediately to Harold's parents, Fred and Mabel, expressing their deepest sympathy.

Easter Sunday passed quietly. The following day was a Bank Holiday and April Fool's Day, but it was too sad a time to play tricks. Alice gave her bedroom a spring clean and Ellen read her letter from Louise Allatt, who had also enclosed a photograph of her husband Harry holding their son Tony in his arms.

Harry was in France with the Royal Flying Corps. He had written to say that the aerodrome was being shelled every day. He said that the German 'Flying Circus' had once regularly outnumbered British planes, but that the opposite was now true.

Their motto was 'Beware of the Hun in the Sun'. They had come a long way since 1914, when there were fewer planes and the pilots had only a revolver to defend themselves. It was a matter of flying as close as you could to an enemy plane and then firing first. The young pilots declined parachutes and if the petrol tank was hit, the plane went up in flames. The flying life of a pilot was sometimes as little as sixteen hours. What the young crews once considered a 'lovely merry war' soon turned out to be a serious and grim task, especially the shock of seeing the corpses strewn all over No Man's Land.

The antics of some of the British airmen were unbelievable. One pilot shot a number of 'Jerry' aircraft down by flying underneath and firing from below. The daily dogfights became a macabre entertainment.

Before the Second Battle of the Somme, 'captive balloons' – known as Blimps – were used by both sides to spy upon one another. The balloons were filled with a hydrogen gas and manned by two courageous men, each with a parachute. They ascended in the balloon and basket armed with a telephone line, to spy upon enemy lines. Invariably, the balloons were shot down. The men would dive out in their parachutes before the basket came thumping down on to the ground. Ellen felt thankful that Harry, Louise's husband, was in hospital in France, well out of the firing line.

The Gibbs' 'billet sons' had an early tea and went off to 'the pictures' in Evesham. Donald went to see the Bancks' son, Norman, in Fladbury.

The day after, Walter sent an application to the local Food Office asking for more sugar, to be preserved.

In early April, Alice had a postcard from her Aunt Polly to say that Raymond had got another stripe and was now a Corporal – but he had written to say that things in Italy were getting 'busy'.

On 5 April, it was Walter and Ellen's wedding anniversary. A postcard with congratulations arrived from her niece, Annie Shenton. Aunt Sophie Davies wrote and so did Polly. Polly told Ellen that her other son John had been called up for a medical examination and had reported to Chislehurst Camp, Windsor, along with eight other men from the Pershore Works. The following day it was heard that John passed his medical, but it was not yet known what service was to claim him. Poor John found himself in khaki in Tidworth, after being sent from Swindon to Canterbury and from there to London. From London he was sent to York and from York back to London again. Kathleen wrote to say that she was weary of being ill and not making much progress in Leamington.

April was the month that saw the Gibbs began life with their new ration cards. Each week, they were allowed 1s 3d worth of fresh meat; 1 lb of sugar; 1½ oz tea; and 4 oz of butter or margarine. Some of the gloom was brightened when Mrs Workman of Holly House in Moor sent a gift of chrysanthemums in pots for Ellen to plant.

Spring was in the air. Arthur Gibbs sent them Rose of Ayr seed potatoes. George Campden was hard at work digging in the top garden, and Walter planted out the Globe Tripoli onions. He mowed the lawns for the first time that year, and Alice cleaned the clothes closets upstairs.

After John's extended tour of the country, Ellen was most surprised to see her nephew appear on the doorstep. He had six days leave and looked smart and well in his khaki uniform. He called back for some dinner after he had been into Evesham. They also had another, less welcome, guest. The irrepressible Thomas Oldham called to tell them that he had bought Manor Farm and its land for £5,000.

The following Sunday, Ellen wrote, 'Very cold day, we are back to winter right enough.'

It was still bitterly cold on Monday, which the last day their billet sons Ben and Edgar would be staying with them for they had finished their hay-loading and had packed up their kitbags ready for their departure by the 7.30 a.m. train the next morning. 'So

Goodbye to our billet sons,' wrote Ellen in her diary. Their next port of call was to be Redditch in Worcestershire.

The Gibbs heard that the air raid on 12 April was near Leamington. Bombs were dropped between there and Coventry. Polly sent them a letter in which she said that the bombs shook the Warmford Hospital where Kathleen was. All the patients who were able enough had to get up. A letter also came for John after he had left for Tidworth, telling him to proceed at once to Gloucester for war work at 'The Gloucester Carriage and Wheel Company'. Polly sent it on to him. Ellen hoped that this would mean that he would be kept in England.

She had heard from her nephew Raymond, who was still in Italy. She also heard that her niece Kathleen was home and staying with her sister Annie Shenton. The doctors had said that she must take things easy for at least two months and that it was unlikely she would ever be able to return to nursing.

Wednesday 17 April was another dreary day. William Harwood brought them three little pigs. He charged three guineas (£3 3s) for each and they really were tiny. As Ellen wrote, they were 'dear little pigs'.

It rained and snowed the following night and there was a sharp frost the following morning, with ice as thick as a penny. The poor plums, Ellen thought, would be badly thinned out. It was another three days before the weather reformed itself. Ellen read in the *Parish Magazine* that 2nd Lieutenant G.K. Stephens of Fladbury Mill had been seriously injured in France and was in a hospital near Manchester. Poor Clara Oldham would be worried about her nephew.

On St George's Day, when Alice and Ellen were spring-cleaning Ellen and Walter's bedroom at the front of the house, they saw about eighty German prisoners being

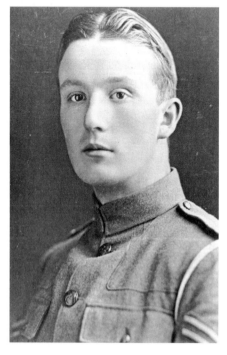

G. K. 'Josh' Stevens of the Warwickshire Yeomanry.

marched up the lane at about 3.30 p.m. They were marching in a military style, accompanied by five guards with fixed bayonets. It was the largest number of Germans that Ellen and Alice had seen.

More reminders of the war came when they heard from Rector Lawson that Ernest Bradley had been killed in action in France, having just returned from Italy.

There was a bit of a war nearer to home when Snip the dog disgraced himself by killing one of Ellen's five beautiful chickens. He had to do penance by being chained up until the remaining four were mature enough to be put into the fowl house.

On Thursday 25 April, they heard the first cuckoo. The bees swarmed, a splendid swarm that Walter handled well. It was early for a swarm of bees. There was an old saying, 'A swarm of bees before May is worth a load of hay but a swarm in July is not worth a fly.'

Ellen sowed some evening scented stock and some Virginia stock.

The time had come to wash through the winter woollens before storing them away for the summer. It was good drying wind, so Ellen conducted a large wash of curtains, cushion covers, and other extras.

On 2 May 1918, Ellen heard from Polly that she and Kathleen, now out of hospital, proposed coming to stay at Bredon View for a few days the following week. Polly had news of Raymond, who was now 'in the line' and up in the mountains of Italy where it was very cold. John was still at Tidworth, having a rough time and keeping busy from daylight to dark.

That same week, Ellen and Walter heard the news that two Moor lads, Walter Wooton and Harry Boulter, had fallen in battle, although it was later found out that Harry was a prisoner of war, and had not been killed.

Walter busied himself in the garden planting lettuce drumhead, early breakfast radish, and some savoy cabbage. Ellen sowed marrow seeds – Early Cream and Ryders Green – and planted a bed of Russian Mammoth sunflower seeds for their poultry to eat.

On 13 May, Ellen was not herself and found that she had not done much work. She had a painful 'gathering' on her gum. It had been grumbling for a day or so, but now it had worsened and had become very painful; her face was quite swollen. She still managed to send away to Pitman Harts for some music to give Alice on her birthday in June. She sent Kathleen a postcard and wrote a long letter to sisters Louise Allatt and Ethel Bland, enclosing some seeds for planting.

The day after, her gum was much better but she feared that her face looked worse. The 'gathering' had broken, which had given her some relief. Alice had kindly risen early and lit the fire and brought Ellen's breakfast up to her, which she greatly appreciated. Despite acute pain, she carried on as normal and did her egg count for the day.

Her face was so improved the following day that she was able to do the washing and rinse out more woollens.

Later, as if the villagers needed any reminding of the fragility of life with the war raging, there was a sad occurrence even closer to home. Mr and Mrs George Haines from Wyre were thrown from their trap as they were driving to their agricultural land through the village. Mr Haines was driving a young colt that began to shy. Mrs Haines was killed and Mr Haines was injured, but there was no indication of how badly hurt he was. Mrs Haines was to be buried on Saturday.

On 22 May, Ellen had a letter returned to her. It was a letter, dated 15 April, sent to Frank Bland. It was marked 'Position evacuated, present position unknown'.

There was better news of Raymond. Polly had a letter from him. He was still in Italy, but now down from the mountains for a few days rest. They also had a letter from Harry Allatt, written on Whitsunday. He said he was in a nice district of France and it reminded him of Worcestershire. He had written the letter sitting under an apple tree.

On Empire Day, 24 May, Alice brought home the news that Ellen and Polly's brother George James had suffered a slight seizure. It had taken the use of his arm and side. Annie Shenton called in to tell them that their uncle was better and the use had come back into his arm. The doctor said that he must stay in bed for a few days and be kept very quiet. Donald was despatched to Peopleton to inquire after his Uncle George.

When he was twenty years old in 1877, their brother George had migrated to America to live with his mother's relatives in Missouri. He was far from happy there and to add to his discomfort, he caught malaria. After eighteen months, he decided to return to England. He had travelled out as a steerage passenger but had found conditions so dreadful that he came back Second Class. On his return, he married Olivia Knight of Pitchill. 'Ollie', as she was known, was a maid at Springhill. By 1892, after the death of William James Sr, George took over as the bailiff at Tilesford Farm.

Towards the end of May, the weather was very hot. Three little village girls called at Bredon View carrying a little maypole and singing a song; Ellen recalled that it was something like this:

All around the Maypole, trip, trip, trot,
See what Maypole we have got,
Ribbons at the bottom, bosses at the top.
All around the Maypole, trip, trip, trot.

Ellen sowed some parsley and camomile seeds but had to give up because of the heat, so she did some mending indoors until she could continue after tea in the cool of the evening. Walter and Ellen planted some kidney beans – better late than never – and a pint of late peas. Donald pulled and bundled up the rhubarb, 5 cwt ready for the jam factory. They were paid 5s per cwt.

On 29 May, Alice received a long letter from Frank Bland, who was in Hooten Pagnell Auxiliary Military Hospital near Doncaster. He had been sent home from France on 14 April to the Military Hospital at Aldershot and through the influence of Mrs Ward-Aldham, his old employer, he was transferred nearer to home, much to his wife Ethel's delight. It was apparent that he had had a very rough time, but he seemed to be much better.

In early June, the heat wave continued. This month the increased rate of postage came into force. It was to cost 1*d* for postcards and 1½*d* for letters. Postage on letters to soldiers serving abroad remained 1*d*.

On Tuesday 4 June, Walter went into Worcester to get parts for a mowing machine and brought home some fresh mackerel that Ellen fried for tea – a delicious treat, for they had not had any fresh fish, only tinned for so long.

In the evening, Walter helped Ellen plant a pint of Laxtonian peas in the top garden. He finished planting a bed of late potatoes, King Edward VII and Evergood varieties.

On Friday 7 June, it was Alice's nineteenth birthday. Walter gave her two shillings and her brother Donald gave her a yard measure in a fancy case with the faces of King George and Queen Mary on it. Kathleen gave her a photograph of herself in nurse's uniform and Aunt Polly gave her a piece of Goss china, a British tank with the Worcester Coat of Arms. Ellen gave her one of John Oxenham's books, *Buchanan Free*, and four pieces of music: *Reminiscences of Rheims*; *Robin's Return*; *The Sailor's Hornpipe*; and *The Return of the Victors*. Alice was very pleased.

The return on 66 lb of gooseberries was 15s.

On Sunday 9 June, Walter and Ellen attended evensong in Fladbury. Will Izod gave them their first few strawberries. As they walked home along Porters Path, they noticed the wheat in the fields 'coming into ear'.

On 12 June, it was a beautiful day. Ellen did the washing. She got all the mangling and ironing done, and she even found time to weed part of the onion bed. She heard that Thomas Oldham, who had been turned down for the Boer War, had now volunteered to fight in this war. He had left Moor the previous day and that very morning Clara Oldham received a postcard from him, 'somewhere in England', to say that he had passed for the Army with flying colours. He was at the Royal Garrison Artillery in Plymouth and hoped to soon be in France. 'We shall see,' wrote Ellen. She recalled the time when Thomas volunteered for the Boer War and he paid for a Bishampton band to come and play him off from Fladbury Station. The following day he quietly returned to the village after the Army declined his services.

Clara Oldham had taken delivery of six German prisoners that day and they were working in the field opposite Bredon View.

The next day, Walter had a letter from Thomas Oldham tendering his resignation as Chairman of the Parish Council, as he was now 'serving His Majesty'.

The month of June saw good news and bad news. Alice began at Mrs Tillman's, the dressmaker in Pershore, as a 'paid hand', earning 12s 6d a week. She worked from 9.00 a.m. until 5.00 p.m. with a half-day on Thursdays.

Reverend Mason, the new clergyman from St Catherine's, arrived and Ellen thought he was a nice, unassuming man. In that same week, Ellen heard from Polly that their brother George had another seizure at about 7.30 p.m. the evening before, taking the use of his left side again, but not his speech. Ellen was upset and disappointed, for he had seemed so well and cheerful last Sunday, when she had seen him. The next day, young Percy Cotterill brought a letter from Polly, saying that George was no worse but could not move without help.

The German prisoners were cherry-picking in Oldham's Orchard. The Gibbs family could hear snatches of German songs and conversation most of the day. Cherries were making £5 to £6 for 'a sieve'. Strawberries were making 1s for every pound until the Government fixed the price at 4d per pound. Ellen wished that they would do the same with cherries. Ellen decided to make some jam with some gooseberries in the afternoon. She was using the wartime recipe for making jam: 'Half a pound of sugar and half a teaspoon of salt to each pound of fruit; then boil the jam for an hour.'

On Sunday 5 July, Alice attended the Annual Flower Service at Fladbury Church, where children and grown-ups alike brought offerings of flowers, many of them quite beautiful. All the flowers were despatched early the next morning by rail to the Rector of Spitalfields, a poor area in the East End of London. The Rector gratefully acknowledged them. He said the flowers were taken to his parish church and distributed to the sick and the poor, giving much pleasure to many. These annual flower offerings were free to the Spitalfields Rector and the proceeds of the collection that Sunday were donated to the sick and needy in Spitalfields.

Early in July, there was an unexpected holiday for Ellen and Alice when Arthur Gibbs invited his Aunt Ellen and Uncle Walter to visit him in Bridgenorth. Walter decided that Ellen and Alice must go for the weekend. Alice seemed to like the idea. Ellen spent some time cooking and cleaning to leave everything straight while she was away.

On 13 July, she wrote in her diary, 'I left this morning – just off to Bridgenorth by the 9.45 a.m. train.' Unfortunately, the connection was not very good and they had to wait in Worcester for the 2.00 p.m. train. They spent most of their four-hour wait very pleasantly in the Worcester Museum and Art Gallery. Arthur met them at Bridgenorth. When they reached Henley House at about 4.00 p.m., they found tea and a nice welcome awaiting them.

Fred and Mabel Gibbs were there. Ellen thought poor Mabel much changed since she had last seen her. She looked so sad but tried to be bright. They were both still stunned by the death of their son Harold in France.

Henley House was very nice, Ellen thought, and beautifully furnished. Arthur's wife Mary was very pleasant and kind and baby Grace was a delightful child. Sunday was rather like a Sunday at home. They attended both morning and evening service at Oldbury Church with Arthur. Despite a busy schedule, Ellen managed to read *At the Foot of the Rainbow* by Gene Stratton Porter during her stay.

On Monday morning, Ellen and Alice went into Bridgenorth to get little presents to take home, which they did the following morning, catching the 12.26 p.m. train to Worcester. Arthur, Mary, and baby Grace waved them off. They arrived at Fladbury at

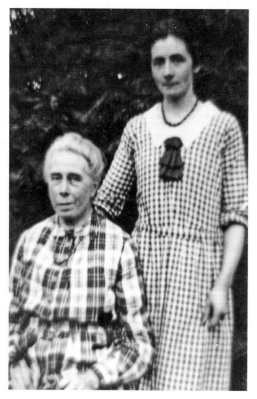

Ellen and Alice Gibbs.

3.20 p.m, having spent a very pleasant few days. Kathleen Wood and Snip the dog were at the station to meet them.

Not being ones to waste time, after tea Ellen and Alice put away their 'glad rags' and changed back into their working clothes so they could pick gooseberries ready for market the following day. In fact, Ellen picked gooseberries with all the time she could spare. For the next couple of days, she was submerged in gooseberries, apples, and plums. She did manage to find time to bake their first apple pudding for dinner one day, and very good it was too.

On Saturday 20 July, there was much thunder and lightning and a heavy downpour that soaked poor Alice on her way home from Pershore.

Kathleen went to see Dr Rushmore in Pershore, who told her that she must give up all thought of going back to nursing. He advised another month's rest and to some brine baths at Droitwich. Only when she was strong enough could she take a light job.

In the midst of all this activity, Miss Maude Robarts, a gracious lady late of Craycombe House, called to see Walter and Ellen. She was staying with Mrs Mary Cartland at Amery Court in Pershore.

Captain Bertram Cartland had been killed in the trenches with his men of the 1st Battalion Worcestershire Regiment during the bitter fighting in France on 27 May. His small daughter, Barbara, and his two sons were left without a father. Mary Cartland bitterly regretted urging her husband to return to France after convalescent leave in England.

On Monday 21 July, Walter decided to go into Evesham on the 3.20 p.m. train. He brought back 2 lb of beef sausages at 1s 3d a pound, and 1lb of tomatoes, also at 1s 3d a pound. Both were a great treat. Ellen had heard that 1lb of tomatoes was anything from 3s 6d to 4s in London. Sausages could be bought without meat coupons, so times were getting better, Ellen thought.

On Saturday 26 July, Donald and Ellen attended a fête at Abbey Manor in Evesham; it proved most enjoyable. Ellen took the train and Donald went on his bicycle. It rained all the way and the sun refused to shine until 2.00 p.m., when it cleared and became beautifully fine for the rest of the day. There was not a dull minute at Abbey Manor; there were lots of attractions: concerts; fancy-step dancing; and Punch and Judy; as well as a man conjuring. The grounds and surroundings were beautiful. Ellen thought it a splendid place for the wounded Tommies to recover.

The following Sunday, 27 July, a very rare event took place. Alice did something to please her father. Rector Lawson called to ask her to play the American organ for the services at Fladbury on Sunday, because Mr. Bancks was ill caused by overwork with Lord Derby's Recruitment Scheme and the running of the school. Ellen thought Alice got through the musical portion of the service beautifully, and she was rewarded by her father's praise. Much to Ellen's amusement, Mr Bancks' exhaustion was described to her by one of the congregation as 'Brain Fag'!

Ellen had a trying week with Walter, who was far from well with gout and liver ailments. Miss Willis Bund brought him a book, *Michael O'Halloran* by Gene Stratton Porter, which diverted him for a while.

He did manage to get up to go to the sale of the late Mr Wagstaff's property in Moor. At one time, the Wagstaff family had been the principal landowners in the area. Walter bought St Catherine's on Blacksmiths Lane on behalf of Mr Francis of The Brooklands, Fladbury, for £450.

Ellen had a letter from Polly to say that son John had walked in unexpectedly the day before on embarkation leave for Egypt. She had heard that her other son Raymond was hoping to be home in a month.

Donald was busy fruit-picking – Lord Grosvenor and Worcester Pearmain apples and Lady Sudely desert apples. He was also gathering Pershore plums; the fixed price for egg plums was £30 per ton.

On 4 August 1918, special Remembrance Day services were held in all the churches in the land, as it was the fourth anniversary of Britain's declaration of war. Donald went to Fladbury Church to hear the sermon given by Reverend J. Ozannie, an Army chaplain and a Captain in the Royal Garrison Artillery. Walter remained in bed after one attempt to rise had failed. Despite the beautiful day, Ellen remained indoors, 'on call' for the invalid.

August Bank Holiday was a fairly good day and a grand fête took place in the Abbey grounds in Pershore in aid of the Prisoner of War Fund. The Gibbs did not attend. It was another tense day with Walter, who again did not leave his bed. His back was bad and his foot very weak; although in comparison with the previous day, Ellen thought him brighter and better.

She tackled the washing and Alice was busy all day cleaning. By Wednesday of that week Walter was back in his forge and Ellen got on with picking the dwarf broad beans for the market, despite the heat. She also bought lamp oil, which was now 2s 1d a gallon.

Ellen heard from William Davies, Aunt Sophie's son. They were taking a holiday in Rhyl and planned to visit Moor for two nights, arriving at Fladbury on the 5.10 p.m. train next Wednesday.

Aunt Sophie Davies was related to Walter's first wife Annie. Both Alice and Donald had been born at her home in Pershore. Aunt Sophie owned a sizeable amount of property in Moor, left to her in Charles Wagstaff's will, in which she was described as 'a servant in his household'.

She owned Whytes Orchard, Old Timbers, and Oakleigh, along with several other cottages in Moor.

It was suspected that Sophie was in fact the natural daughter of Elizabeth Fryer, housekeeper to Charles Wagstaff, the farmer, fruit grower, and market gardener of Moor. As a baby Sophie was 'adopted' and brought up with Annie's father's family at Whytes Orchard in Moor. When she was in her teens, she returned to live with Elizabeth Fryer and Charles Wagstaff until the latter's death.

Ellen heard from Edwin Gibbs in Malmsbury. He proposed coming to stay, along with his children Willie, Dorrie, and Edgar, all travelling on their cycles on the same day that Sophie and her son were to depart.

With temperatures soaring, poor Ellen spent all morning and all afternoon preparing for her numerous visitors.

Aunt Sophie and her son and daughter-in-law arrived at teatime. Ellen thought they all looked well, especially Aunt Sophie, who was eighty years of age. Her husband James had died the year before, aged ninety-seven. He was brought back to his native Pershore from London to be buried. For most of their married life James and Sophie had lived at the bottom of Bridge Street in Pershore.

James Davies was an interesting man. Born in 1820, he was employed as a letter carrier. His contract of employment was signed by Lord Clarendon, who was Post Master General during Robert Peel's first term as Prime Minister in 1834/35.

He could remember the last outbreak of cholera in Pershore. He retired at the age of seventy-five and drew a pension of 11s a week for twenty-two years.

James Davies was a widower with a grown-up daughter when he married Aunt Sophie, and he was not considered a good catch. Apparently, James had less than perfect eyesight; in less polite society, he would have been described as cross-eyed. When Sophie indicated her intention of marrying James, Elizabeth Fryer, her mother, replied, 'Ah well, he ain't much to look at. Sophie will be able to do whatever 'er likes for he'll never see what 'er's up to.' James eventually went blind, but he remained a good speller; he had been a star turn in his youth at the Pershore spelling bees.

The Great War passed him by. He could not comprehend food rationing. He would take several spoonfuls of sugar with his tea. To every entreaty to use less sugar, he would turn a deaf ear saying, in a broad Worcestershire accent, 'War or no War, I must ha' mi sugar!'

Ellen had barely an hour to rush around, for as soon as Aunt Sophie and her party had left Bredon View, Walter's younger brother Edwin arrived with his three children. They had cycled all day from Wiltshire, starting off at 7.15 a.m. The children had coped well with the journey and seemed quite fresh, if dusty and travel-stained.

The following day, Walter and Edwin went to Pershore where they met Raymond Wood. He had arrived home from Italy the night, before, much to Polly and Ellen's delight.

Monday was a beautiful day and Raymond came over in the morning and stayed until dinner. Ellen was really thrilled to see her favourite nephew. He looked thinner

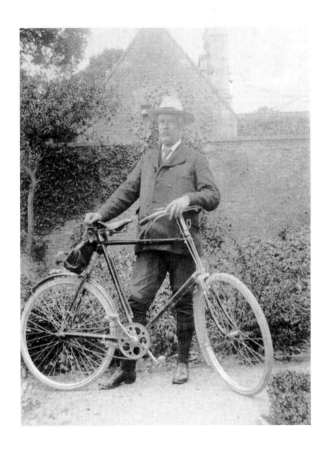

Edwin Gibbs with his bicycle.

but otherwise well and bright. Edwin and Raymond went to Pershore with Alice in the morning and in the afternoon Edwin and his young folk went to Evesham, where they hired a boat and went on the river.

On Tuesday, it was hotter than ever. Edwin and the boys went to Peopleton to see Polly and George. They took their tea with them.

While her guests were away, Ellen did the washing that had accumulated. She even managed to send off the *Evesham Journal*, containing reports of the harvest, to Florrie in Canada.

Wednesday was a scorcher, so Edwin and Donald and the boys headed down to the River Avon and had a dip. Raymond and his sister Annie called in the evening and they had a 'nice interesting chat' with their Aunt Ellen. Annie mentioned that Raymond was 'walking out' with a local girl from Bishampton. Selina was her name and she was acting head housemaid at Wood Norton Hall.

Thursday was a little cooler, with more breezes. Edwin and the children started off for Pershore – or so Ellen thought. Instead they went to Worcester, landing back at Bredon View at 5.00 p.m. They had been to the cathedral and the museum and had a fine old time. Unfortunately, Ellen had prepared dinner for everyone at noon, so the visitors' dinner was waiting on the table all afternoon. However, they were ready and hungry when they returned home and merrily rolled dinner and tea into one.

It was a nice fine day on Saturday. Walter had some warnings of gout but happily for everyone, it passed off. In the afternoon, Edwin and his young folk went into Evesham, getting back for tea at 8.00 p.m. They were full of excitement and had a present for Ellen – and such a present, a tin of salmon and a bottle of French olives. Donald's purchase of some tomatoes at 1s per pound was quite an anticlimax.

After a Sunday of churchgoing, Edwin, Ellen and Walter were busy gathering things together ready for their visitors' departure the next morning. The rain kept off long enough for them to ride away on their 'iron horses' at 10.00 a.m. Ellen spent the rest of the day tidying up. On Wednesday 28 August, Ellen heard that Edwin and the children had arrived home safely.

Ellen received a postcard from John Wood. He told her that they were 'progressing' with their journey, but that it was 'very hot'. Raymond called in to say goodbye. He had a bit of dinner with them and then away he went home – before returning to France (they supposed) on Friday. The Gibbs family gathered at the top of the front path to get a clear view of the railway line that lay at the far side of the large field across the lane from Bredon View. They looked out for the train passing through Lower Moor and everyone gave a last goodbye wave to Raymond, waving as many tea towels as they could muster. Ellen finished the ironing and made some marrow jam, which was lovely. Annie and Tom Shenton called in the evening and stayed for supper.

The following Friday, Alice did not get home until 9.00 p.m. that night. She had been working late for three nights, getting the work 'done up' before the holiday that was to begin on Monday.

On Sunday 1 September, Walter and Ellen went to evensong at Fladbury after a lovely walk across the fields – nearly all the corn had been 'carried'.

On Monday 2 September, there was a cold wind all day, and the people were beginning to say, 'We have done with summer'.

Ellen and Walter went into Evesham where Ellen bought thirty yards of white and green casement cloth for the windows. The white was 2s a yard and the green was 1s

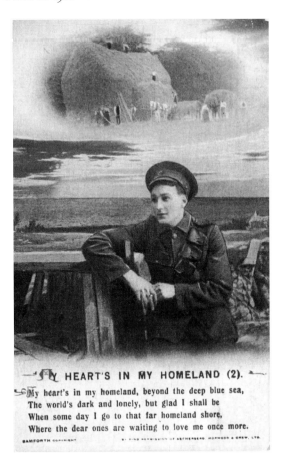

HEART'S IN MY HOMELAND (2).

My heart's in my homeland, beyond the deep blue sea,
The world's dark and lonely, but glad I shall be
When some day I go to that far homeland shore,
Where the dear ones are waiting to love me once more.

A postcard of the type Ellen received from John Wood. Many were decorated with romantic lyrics. The soldier is smoking and daydreaming about harvest in rural England.

a yard. It made quite a hole in her £5 note. On the second day of her 'holidays', Alice began making the curtains.

Ellen was feeling far from well again; her limbs ached and she felt she had a chill inside her. Despite this, she struggled on with the washing and managed to get it dry. A postcard from Polly cheered her a little. Raymond had crossed the Channel safely and was feeling fit and well in Le Havre.

On Thursday, it was so chilly that they had to light a fire in the kitchen.

On Friday, Alice 'autumn-cleaned' the sitting room. In the evening, she put on the new cretonne chair covers that she had made. They looked very nice.

On Saturday, during the first week of her holiday, Alice went into Evesham to buy another six yards of white casement cloth. She bought a raincoat for herself for £1 19s 11d.

Walter had an interesting letter from Mr Bancks. The Fladbury schoolmaster was spending a holiday in Liverpool with his wife and family.

He said that on Wednesday the liner *Mauritania* had landed a huge contingent of our new allies. The American troops, he thought, all looked fit enough to 'keep Fritz in a pippy mood'. He said that there were several Yankee camps up there and American fighting men could be met at every turn. He said that the naval men wore a peculiar white cap that reminded him of a pork pie.

Walter attended a meeting in Fladbury and came back to say that there was little chance of any charity coal being distributed to the poor and needy in the parish for the coming winter, as stocks were so low. He also told Ellen that Lieutenant Jack Godfrey had been gassed again, but was recovering, and that Edgar Byrd was back in hospital after losing his left arm in the fighting in Palestine. Despite the steadily growing hope of victory, the daily death blows continued to fall on local families.

Meanwhile, the German prisoners were digging up Mrs Oldham's potatoes all day in the field opposite Bredon View.

The following Monday, a 'radiant' start ended up as a wet and windy day. Walter went into Evesham on the 6.00 p.m. train and came home in a rather merry mood with Mr Henry Rimmell of Throckmorton. Both men were in sparkling form. Walter did not get into the house until a good bit after 9.00 p.m., just as his family were beginning to wonder what had become of him.

On Tuesday, after thoroughly cleaning the sitting room, Alice put up the new curtains.

On Friday 13 September, Ellen thought they were in 'luck's way', for Ned Righton from Fladbury called and left a brace of partridges for them. Polly came over to Bredon View to stay with Alice and Donald while she and Walter went for a welcome break to Malvern for the weekend.

Saturday dawned dull, but the weather cleared up as Walter and Ellen left on the 10.00 a.m. train from Fladbury Station to Malvern, twenty miles away. They had to change at Foregate Street, Worcester, as well as Shrub Hill, only a mile or so further down the line. They arrived at Great Malvern at 11.30 a.m. and were fortunate enough to find comfortable lodgings with Mrs Doughty, of Ivy Mount, St Annie's Road, at 3s 6d per night with 'use of the sitting room and attendance'.

After they had eaten the packed the lunch that they had brought with them from home, they went out on the hill as far as St Annie's Well, returning to tea at five. At 7.30 p.m. they went to the pictures at the Assembly Rooms. It was very good, Ellen thought – a newsreel and a version of Jules Verne's *Twenty Thousand Leagues Under the Sea*, which they both enjoyed. That night it rained and the next day was rather dull and hazy. After breakfast, Walter and Ellen went to the 11.00 a.m. service at the Great Malvern Priory and in the afternoon they attended an organ recital.

Their evening was taken up by a visit to the Congregational Place of Worship. Ellen thought the service was very good, but she missed the 'dignity' of a Church of England. To add a bit of excitement to their holiday, there were five young bright and lively girls staying at Ivy Mount and sharing the sitting room with them. Ellen thought they were a merry party.

Despite a dull Monday morning, Walter and Ellen decided that after breakfast they would attempt to get to the top of the Worcestershire Beacon. They found it enveloped in thick cloud with a strong wind almost forcing them off their feet. In the afternoon they took a less strenuous stroll to the Wych Pass, a lovely walk with good views on the way.

In the evening, they went to an enjoyable concert in the public gardens, which were especially beautiful. It was most pleasant to sit and feast their eyes on the beauty of their surroundings. Alas, the next day after breakfast, Walter went to the station to enquire about the trains for going home and Ellen did a bit of souvenir shopping for the 'home birds'. They left Malvern station at 5.50 p.m., arriving home by the 8.00 p.m. train. It took a long time to travel those 20 miles, especially as they could see the Malvern Hills from their bedroom window at Bredon View. They had spent a very pleasant time, doing all right for food with the help of a few provisions taken from home.

Polly heard that her son John had arrived in Alexandria in Egypt on 28 August. Ellen wrote, rather tersely, that Thomas Oldham had arrived home on leave, 'full of gas'. The 'drinking man's drinking man' was to return to Plymouth soon and was expecting to be sent to Egypt or Malta, or so he had informed Walter.

On 26 September, Polly heard that Raymond was back in action in France. Hearts sank at the news, but they hoped it was for some good purpose.

They heard that Kathleen's friend, Sergeant Fred Davis, had died of his wounds in a French hospital. Poor Kathleen was staying with her sister Annie in Pinvin for a week to help recover from the shock.

Donald received a photo postcard of Frank Bland and some of the men of his company, and it pleased him very much. The Gibbs household also received their coal ration papers. They were allowed six tons for the year, for the blacksmith's shop and house. Walter went to Evesham and came home armed with some tomatoes at 1s 3d a pound and sausages at 1s 6d a pound. Ellen made some pumpkin jam and Walter 'took' the honey that evening, not a lot, about 10 lb.

For the Harvest Thanksgiving service, Donald took some potatoes and apples to church. The offerings of fruit and vegetables from the parish were to be sent to the Pershore Cottage Hospital and the Worcester Ophthalmic Hospital.

Sadly, there was news of another death, but not as a result of the war. They heard that Mrs Clarke had died. The poor woman was only forty-two years old and had left eleven children motherless. She had worked very hard for her family and was considered a first-rate laundress. The news cast gloom over Moor. Her funeral was arranged for

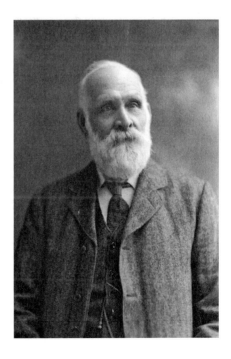

Walter Gibbs.

the following Wednesday, Ellen thought September had not proved a golden one that year for anyone.

On 2 October, Ellen reported that milk was 7d a quart and was advised that one should go and 'fetch it', for if you had it delivered, it cost 8d a quart.

Mrs Oldham's milk cart was driven by Bertha, a Belgian refugee and Clara Oldham's right hand. Previously, young Mary Jones from Bridge Street in Moor had delivered the milk, going as far as Cropthorne, over the Jubilee Bridge from Fladbury. She had been frightened once by some gypsies, who were by the bridge demanding milk. She only got by them by promising to give them some milk on her way back. The poor girl was so scared that she returned in the milk cart to Moor via Pershore and Wyre, a nine-mile detour.

Ellen noted that there was a most successful rummage sale for the Nursing Fund in Moor Parish Room. Most people wore old clothes year after year because the price and quality of new clothes were so unsatisfactory. A good selection of clothes had been donated for the sale. They hoped that people were willing to pay a little more than they would have done before the war. Alice took some persuading to help man the tables piled high with clothes, for as the doors were opened, there was a terrifying stampede of women to get to the bounty.

There was always a rush for Elizabeth Smyth's donation of rummage. She gave lots of silk stockings that were snipped by scissors at the top for maximum comfort. All they needed was a quick sewing-up and they could be worn.

Elizabeth Smyth bought a great deal of her clothes from the exclusive Warwick House in Malvern. Good-quality clothes also came from Mrs Janet Bomford. Some of the Officers at Craycombe House donated clothes, too. The sale raised the magnificent amount of £25.

On Thursday 3 October, Alice took a trip into Evesham to be photographed. While she was there, she chose the book *The Elusive Pimpernel* as a birthday present for her father, and ordered James W. Gerard's *My Four Years in Germany* for Ellen to give to Walter. She bought some wool to knit herself some stockings and started them as soon as she got home.

Ellen had a postcard from Ethel Bland to say that Frank was coming home on leave, though he had to report to Southampton in a week. The family feared he was to be in foreign service again.

Polly wrote, saying that John had written from Egypt. He said that when they washed their clothes it was so hot that they could wash, dry, and put them back on in less than two hours! They were soon to journey 200 miles up the line, but had enjoyed their four days in the Mediterranean, which was as smooth and calm as the River Severn. Raymond, meanwhile, had done something to his right hand and could scarcely use it, so the family hoped it would mean a bit of rest in a place of safety for him.

As for Walter, he was ailing again. He had a sore throat and was developing a nasty cold. He went to bed for two days, but help was at hand. While at a funeral in Pershore, the rector kindly purchased Mr Smith's Anti-Cold Tablets for the ailing Walter. The family had heard that the 'flu epidemic was particularly bad in London. Ellen hoped that it would stay there and not affect the rural areas.

Sunday 6 October was a day of high winds. Donald returned from Fladbury Church that morning with a book of music from Mrs Smyth, 'Hours of Pleasure', for Alice.

Ellen belonged to the Church Sewing Guild. Every year, every member made seven useful garments, which were sent to London and distributed to needy families across the country. Donald took Ellen's promised garments to the Rectory, a local collection point.

Sunday 13 October 1918 was Walter's sixty-first birthday. He was well enough to go out for a little in the morning sun and was well pleased with his presents. Louise had written and sent him a photograph of herself and one of Ethel. Ellen thought they were very good.

Monday 14 October was dull and cold and Ellen found it depressing and disappointing. She did the washing but there was no chance of getting it dry. On 17 October, Ellen had a fire in the sitting room, the first that autumn, so that Alice could use the piano and 'have a bit of music'.

Saturday was a lovely day and Ellen noted the autumnal tints in the trees. The surrounding hillsides were full of the most glorious hues of gold and amber, especially the wooded area by the Wood Norton Estate.

Walter spent a week in the house, 'clerking', as he did not feel up to working at the forge. He had been out for little walks around the house with one of the old hens as his companion. The hen followed him around at heel, like a dog. Ellen noticed that his cold 'keeps bad' on his chest, despite Alice cycling to Pershore to fetch him a bottle of medicine from the chemist. However, Ellen was delighted to record that Walter's 'clerking' during the time that he was confined to the house had been a success. He had managed to get all the work entered into the ledger and it was actually up to date!

It was at this time that Ellen and Walter decided that Alice should give up her job. They wanted her to leave in the middle of November, as she was to stay at home and help her stepmother. How Alice felt about this move there is no mention, but she cannot have been too happy. It fell to poor Alice to cycle into Pershore and inform Mrs Tillman herself that she would no longer be working for her.

The hated chimney sweep was expected towards the end of October and Ellen spent a long time dust-sheeting everything in readiness. He arrived at 8.00 a.m. and swept the kitchen and back kitchen chimneys, creating more cleaning up for Ellen after he had gone.

Polly wrote to say how worried she was about her boys. She had heard nothing from John and only had a few letters from Raymond – dated 21 October, just before the last offensive began.

News was also received at Peopleton that Jim Hunt had been seriously wounded on 24 October and was too ill to be visited. They feared the worst.

On 30 October, Annie Shenton called on her way home from Craycombe with an evening paper containing the good news that Turkey had surrendered to the Allies. Ellen cheered, 'Hip Hurrah!'

The last day of October 1918 was a lovely mild day of sunshine and Donald went into Evesham to have his photograph taken, and to have his collection of *The Boy's Own Paper* bound.

By Sunday 3 November, the winds had left precious few leaves upon the trees. It was a dull and wet day and much to Ellen's concern, Alice's chill had turned into the dreaded Spanish 'Flu. Walter went to get her some medicine from Pershore. Mr Smith, the chemist, told him to keep Alice in bed for a few days on a 'sloppy diet'.

On 6 November, a sharp frost was followed by a lovely day of sunshine, Alice began to improve but by an icy 7 November, Donald had come down with the 'flu.

Walter and Ellen sent for Dr Asham, who arrived at about 3.30 p.m. They were glad to be told that there was nothing seriously wrong with Alice or Donald, but that they should both be kept in their beds.

The weather soon turned to a 'duck's frost'. It rained a lot in the night and was very windy but it was bright during the day. Alice and Donald were recovering well from their influenza. Not so, poor twenty-three-year-old Florence Cowley from Moor, who died that day.

On Monday 11 November 1918, Ellen wrote about the 'glorious news' of peace terms being signed by the Germans. The Rector called just after dinner to say that he was going to Pershore. But there was no need; they could hear Pershore Abbey's bells ringing out as they stood at the top of the front path of the house. They knew then that the good news had come.

Walter and Ellen soon had their Union Jack flying from their front bedroom window at Bredon View. The Fladbury bells were ringing out at 3.00 p.m. and Walter went to a service of thanksgiving in Fladbury that evening. Ellen imagined how many thankful hearts there would be that night, and how many sad ones. She wondered how long it would be before the boys started to come home for good.

Walter returned from the service to say that it had been very impressive and that the church was absolutely packed. They sang the National Anthem and hymns ancient and modern: number 165, 'O God, Our Help in Ages Past', number 435, 'Hark the Sound of Holy Voices', and hymn 379, 'Now Thank We All Our God'.

The following day was bright and frosty. Alice and Donald were recovering from the 'flu, still under the doctor's care but doing well. Ellen tackled the washing in the afternoon after the doctor had departed. She had no desire to receive him in the morning with soapy hands and wearing her apron, although she always removed her apron before answering the front door.

On the night of Wednesday 13 November, there was a torchlight procession on Bredon Hill between 8.00 p.m. and 9.00 p.m. The Gibbs family watched from Walter and Ellen's bedroom window at the front of the house. They had an uninterrupted view of Bredon Hill. It was exciting to see the long dots of light slowly moving up and along the top of the hill.

Alice Hodges called on the morning of 14 November, telling them that Peopleton was full of excitement with the good news of the armistice, but that the Wood family were anxious about Raymond, as they had not heard from him since 29 October.

The Rector told them that 'three of our lads' who had been prisoners of war were now home: George Martin from Germany; Ralph Meadows from Turkey; and poor Fred Foster who was taken by the Germans in August 1914. How they must have suffered, thought Ellen. The Rector went on to say they were fairly well, all things considered.

Sadly, they also heard that May Hughes had died from influenza, aged just twenty-seven.

By Sunday 17 November 1918, things were back to normal in the Gibbs household. Alice played the harmonium at Moor Church as usual. It was a very nice service taken by the latest curate, Reverend Parret. Walter and Ellen very much enjoyed the hearty service and the splendid address.

Ellen talked afterwards to the Guide Mistress, who was planning to march her troop of guides into Evesham, where they would take their place in the Grand Victory Parade the next day. Although it was a long march for them, she told Ellen that she thought they might catch 'the 'flu germ' if they travelled by train. Most of the girls were disappointed at missing the treat of going on the train to Evesham.

On Monday 18 October, Alice had cast off all invalid ways and turned out her bedroom thoroughly. Donald had gone to Fladbury Mill to fetch some corn for the fowls.

The Spanish 'Flu continued to rage through the country parish. Miss Janet Bomford of Springhill was very ill and had a temperature of 104 degrees Fahrenheit; Mr Sidney Sharp of Wyre Mill was seriously ill with pneumonia; Michael Andrews of Wyre, aged nineteen, died from the 'flu only months after the death of his soldier brother, Private Joseph Andrews, in Egypt. The Andrews family had already lost a young daughter through illness. Ellen could hardly bear to think how the family were bearing such dreadful blows.

Nearly all the Prussian prisoners of war at Craycombe camp were down with influenza. Twenty-six were suffering from pneumonia. Four of the Austrian prisoners had died at Bowbrook House camp in Peopleton. It had been decided to bury them in Peopleton Churchyard.

The Gibbs also received a postcard from Edwin in Malmsbury, to say he was the only member of his family that was well. All their children were down with influenza, and his wife Annie was very poorly.

Louise, Walter's sister in London, wrote to say that she had the old-fashioned influenza and her husband John was very poorly with the Spanish 'Flu. Because of the severity of the epidemic, Walter and Ellen had to cancel the annual supper they gave for the handbell ringers.

On 20 November, Ellen had a postcard from Polly to say that she had good news of Raymond. He had written on the 11 November to say that he was so pleased and excited by the armistice and felt glad to be alive after all they had been through. He said that they did not feel like the same men now that there were no 'red hot oranges' falling around them. He said that he was well and in good billets near Cambrai.

On Friday 22 November, Ellen made one very small jar of mincemeat to put away for Christmas.

On 23 November, Walter took a trip into Worcester and brought back with him a bag full of nice things; fish, cakes, and tomatoes. Ellen thought that things were looking up. He bought her a pretty blouse, for a birthday present. She had a letter of birthday wishes and a pretty card from Polly, as well as a postcard from Alice Hodges.

Sunday 24 November was Ellen's fifty-third birthday and her sister Polly's sixtieth birthday. Alice gave Ellen a delightful surprise that morning with her gift of the book that Ellen had wanted for a long time, *Flower of the Dusk* by Myrtle Reed. Donald was more down-to-earth and gave her a dusting brush and a satirical postcard of the German Emperor.

Ellen received a nice letter from Ethel with a photograph of herself and one of Louise and Tony. Ethel's husband Frank was home on a week's leave, returning to Southampton that very day; he expected to be sent to France again. Harry Allatt, Louise's husband, was working in Germany.

Ellen heard from the Guide Mistress after church that evening that despite her precautions, nearly all her guides had gone down with the 'flu.

Ellen also heard from Florrie and Archie in Canada. They had been bidden by her father, Ellen's brother George, to return home to Peopleton and help with the farm. She said they hoped to be in England before this time next year.

On Saturday 30 November, Donald told Ellen that Polly had received a postcard from John telling her that he was ill in hospital in Alexandria. He didn't know what was wrong. Ellen had a quiet evening at home, reading her new book.

Ellen had been having some trouble with a tooth and went to the dentist in Evesham on the 9 December to have the tooth 'stopped', or filled – and to do some Christmas shopping. Alice Hodges went with her and went off to shop while Ellen was at the dentist. They met up later with Walter, who came in on the afternoon train. They returned home together.

After tea, Alice Hodges packed a Christmas parcel for her husband Fred, ready to send the next day.

On 12 December, there was a long letter from John Wood who had been in hospital in Alexandria at the time of writing, 18 November. He had mild malaria fever but was improving. He was allowed a bottle of stout a day. He was near Damascus when taken ill. Ellen sent a postcard to Polly to say that she had heard from him. She also received a souvenir card, 'Greetings from Egypt', from John.

Around this time, Ellen was driven in fine style in Mr Godfrey's car up to Throckmorton to record her vote for the first time. (Women over the age of thirty got their vote in 1918.) It was and always would be a Conservative stronghold, whether you liked it or not. But what a day to cherish! A landmark for Women's Liberation. A pity, Ellen wrote, that it had taken a war to bring it about.

The following Monday, Alice went into Evesham to do her Christmas shopping and Walter went to the Rectory to go over the Charity Coal accounts with the Rector. Ellen made two small Christmas puddings.

That same day, they heard with great sadness that Henry Rimmell of Throckmorton was very ill with influenza, which had turned into pneumonia. This was sometimes called 'the old people's friend', but Henry Smith Rimmell was only fifty-six years old.

Henry Rimmell died on the night of 19 December. Rector Lawson said it was regrettable that the dreaded influenza had carried off the one man to whom everyone looked up to. 'What a great loss his death would be to his loving family and the parish,' he said. 'As an employer he was fair and just; as a farmer he was shrewd and much respected; as a friend and neighbour he was thoroughly kind.'

There was no doubt that Harry Rimmell's death would cast a great cloud of gloom upon Throckmorton, especially as his wife and two daughters would be leaving their home, for none of them had any farming experience. Their home, Lower Farm, one of the two large farmhouses in Throckmorton, was a large, roomy house with a sheltered, walled garden, built originally for a Mr Buckle.

When Mr Buckle died, Henry Rimmell's father, who lived at Pebworth, bought the farm for Henry, his newly-wed son, more affectionately known as 'Harry'.

The ever-sympathetic but practical Ellen wrote a letter of condolence to Mrs Rimmell and her daughters, Daisy and Kate. As usual, Donald played his part as errand boy and took the letter up to 'Throggy' after breakfast the next morning.

Henry Rimell's funeral took place at 2.30 p.m. on Monday 22 December at Throckmorton Church. Walter and Ellen attended and found that the church was full, mostly with Henry's farm labourers, village men, and farmers and gentlemen of the neighbourhood. Poor Mrs Rimmell bore it very well but the girls, Kathleen and Daisy, were not well enough to attend. There was a lovely wreath from them and their mother, which said, 'Until the day breaks and the shadows flee away.' The choir sang 'Rock of Ages', and it was all very sad.

Ellen spent Christmas Eve in food preparation. She used the small amount of mincemeat to make one large plate pie and two smaller pies on saucers, one for Alfred Huckfield and one for George Barley in Moor.

Walter went into Evesham in the afternoon to collect his suit and buy presents for the family. He returned on the 7.55 p.m. train with some additions to the Christmas fare; a pork pie, some sausages, and a cake.

Christmas Day 1918 was a lovely, bright day. Alice and Ellen went to Moor for Holy Communion at 9.45 a.m. The Rector took the service.

Polly, Walter, and Donald went to Fladbury for the morning service and Polly, Alice, Walter, and Ellen went to Moor Church in the afternoon for a nice, bright service, taken by Reverend Parrett.

Donald went over to Fladbury to spend the evening with Norman Bancks at the schoolhouse.

Donald had given Ellen another Boots diary for 1919. Alice gave her a book, *The Babes in the Wood* by B. Cromer. More practical than romantic, Walter gave her a pair of galoshes. It was a quietly happy Christmas Day. 'Peace on Earth, and Good Will to all men,' wrote a thankful Ellen.

Boxing Day was cold and arrived with a frost. Walter commenced his 'clerking'. Ellen received a newspaper sent by Florrie from Victoria in Vancouver Island, where they were living for the winter. She had a nice quiet day reading *The Babes in the Wood*.

On 28 December, it was a fine, very mild day. Ellen noticed that the young almond tree by the privet hedge was in bud. A parcel arrived that morning from Coventry. It was from Aunt Sophie and cousins Willie and Gertie, posted on 23 December. It contained a nice book each for Alice and Donald and a Keswick calendar for Walter and Ellen. Ellen also received a note from Jesse Shervington thanking her for their Christmas gifts, saying, 'The remembrances of old friends sweetens life'.

That evening, Donald was despatched to Fladbury to find out the election results. He came home with the good news that Conservative MP Mr Eyres-Monsell was returned with a majority of 4,645. 'Hip-Pip!' wrote Ellen. The Government was now a coalition between the Conservatives and Prime Minister David Lloyd George's Liberals.

Sunday 29 December 1918 was a Day of Remembrance before God of those who had given their lives in the war. The churches of Fladbury and Moor held beautiful services. Reverend Parrett preached at Moor from the words, 'Be thou faithful unto death and I will give thee a crown of life.' The offerings were given to the hard-pressed Red Cross.

The last day of 1918 was a bright day with a very cold wind. Donald Gibbs was progressing with his lettuce-planting in the cold frame. Alice Gibbs went to Pershore in the afternoon and came back with the sad news that Maurice Saunders had died. He was a prisoner of war in Turkey. It was very sad for his family, as the other prisoners were returning to Pershore that evening and until recently they had such good hopes of welcoming Maurice home. Ellen wrote to her brother George and sister Polly with New Year wishes.

They had got through another year together, but what would 1919 bring for the Gibbs family?

Chapter Six

The Aftermath

Adapted from the 1919 diary of Ellen Gibbs of Bredon View, Lower Moor near Pershore, Worcestershire.

The year did not come in very gloriously as regards to the weather. Ellen wrote, 'It was a dull morning turning to a downpour of very cold rain in the afternoon. It was followed by a very wild and windy night'.

The post was interesting; a pretty postcard from Polly and a postcard from Harry Allatt of Bonn in Germany, expressing his best wishes. He wrote from a large aerodrome near Bonn, a few miles the other side of the Rhine River. He said they had been doing a lot of moving around lately and that he was longing for home.

Friday 3 January was a fine day. Donald and Ellen were weighed that day. Donald weighed 10 st and Ellen weighed 9 st 12 lb. For the first time, Ellen noted, he had beaten her.

The following day, they awoke to a bright, white world.

The Gibbs household was saddened to hear that Mrs Morris of Hill Furze had died in the night from the Spanish 'Flu. The poor soul had seen all her five sons serve in the Army throughout the war and then, finally, when the anxious years of waiting were over, influenza had claimed her. She was to be buried on the 8 January.

On Thursday 9 January, Alice encounter heavy storms of rain during her ride into Pershore for margarine and suet. At Alice's expense, Ellen could not resist writing, 'and got dripping coming home!'

It was a red-letter day for the hens, not the pullets. One of the hens laid an egg for the first time for months. Ellen noted that paraffin was much cheaper; it had dropped from 2s 2d to 1s 7d per gallon.

Annie Shenton spent the day with Ellen as her husband Tom had gone to Banbury to get his new teeth. Ellen spotted lots of snowdrops springing up in the garden.

Ellen heard from Polly via Percy Cotterill; she had received a letter from Raymond in France telling her of their good Christmas and New Year fare. They were served with turkey and plum pudding and wine. He said that they often get good suppers now, but for all that, he was longing for England and home.

Alfred Bomford of Springhill came in with Walter at 5.00 p.m. and stayed for tea. Walter and Donald went to Worcester on Saturday on the 10 a.m. train and returned on the 5.15 p.m. They had explored the cathedral that Donald so loved.

Today was also Raymond Wood's twenty-eighth birthday. Ellen prayed that it would be the last that he would spend in France. Alice and Kathleen went over to Pinvin to help Annie celebrate her thirtieth birthday. They took some music and songs with them and they all had a pleasant time. When they returned, Ellen was given the good news that Raymond was now a Sergeant.

On Friday 17 January, they had a postcard from Harry Allatt, who was now in Cologne. Ellen also noted that their beef from Mr Tolley that week was 1s 11d per pound and commented that this was the highest price they had paid since pre-war days.

On Thursday 23 January, there was a very sharp frost followed by a bright crisp day. Ellen and Alice went to Evesham by the 3.20 p.m. train, principally to get Ellen a shower-proof coat. She was pleased with the one she bought at Hamilton and Bells for three guineas (£3 3s). They went to have a look at the Ionian cross, erected in memory of Simon de Montfort. It was nice, but they did not like it as much as the one at Fladbury; it was a different style altogether.

The next day it was freezing. The Rector called to ask Walter to attend a preliminary meeting at Fladbury Parish Room the following evening, to discuss what form the village memorial should take, if one was to be erected. Walter, with his sense of duty to the village, attended the meeting. It was arranged that they would have another meeting in all four villages in the parish. Mr Newman of Tilesford suggested that Fladbury Cross would be a good position, but the Wyre people were in favour of having a memorial all of their own.

Walter commented that it looked like the subject of the war memorial was going to cause a war of its own. A few days later, however, he attended yet another meeting at Moor Parish Room. It was fairly well attended and it was unanimously agreed that Fladbury Cross would be the prestigious site.

On Wednesday, Polly wrote to Ellen to say that she was feeling the cold badly and was in desperate straits for coal. She had heard from John that he had left the Abyssinia Schools hospital after plenty of good fare at Christmas and was now in a convalescence camp.

On the 30 January, Ellen received a postcard from Ethel Bland to say that her husband Frank had got his discharge and was home 'for GOOD'. He had begun to work again for Mrs Ward-Aldham as an estate agent's clerk, and found himself very busy.

Meanwhile, Walter had a bad cold. He walked over to the Rectory that evening to go over the Amalgamated Charities with the Rector. The roads were in a very slippery state and he had a 'sit down' on the way home along Porters Path, momentarily losing his lantern and some of his papers. Fortunately, he said that he had done himself no harm. Ellen and Alice looked at each other, barely repressing smiles, and chorused how glad they were that he was unharmed.

The next day, Donald battled his way to Fladbury to collect Ellen's working boots. Mr Moseley had done them up well. He had soled and heeled them, and patched and toe-capped one of them. He charged her 5s.

Rector Lawson called in the afternoon, followed by Mrs Lidsey, who came to ask them if they would like a hare. Mr Lidsey had shot two the day before.

The last day of January was not a good one for Ellen.

It was sleeting in the morning and extremely cold as they prepared for a morning visit from the sweep. Much to Ellen's great indignation, he did not turn up. When Alice went into Pershore that afternoon to collect some margarine, she called in on Mrs Danish, the sweep's wife, who told Alice he could not come before the following Monday morning. All the preparations and waiting had been in vain.

Ellen was extremely annoyed that he had not had the decency to let her know. To make matters worse, Walter had succumbed to his cold and was in bed all day.

Mrs Lidsey arrived with the promised hare. Much to Ellen's indignation, she was charged 10s for it.

Mr Spencer Workman from Holly House walked along the lane in the afternoon to see Walter and tell him the latest news about the war memorial. There had been a meeting at Fladbury the night before, when they decided on a cross. The Fladbury people wanted to have it erected on their village green and the Moor representatives presumed that there it would be, for Fladbury folk invariably had the last say. The Wyre people, on the other hand, were going to have their own war memorial.

The first Sunday in February was a dull, raw day. Alice stayed at home with Ellen and Walter, who got up for a while after lunch. Donald was the only one to venture to Fladbury Church in the evening.

Ellen wrote to Florrie in Canada and enclosed a card for their son Bobbie's birthday, which was in March. Florrie and Archibald led a hard life in Canada, especially in the winter, when it was bitterly cold. The men worked very long hours and the women worked hard keeping house – mistress and maid together. There was less class distinction in Canada. Ellen wondered how they would fare when they came back to England and once more encountered the 'know your place and stay there' attitude.

Mr Daniels the sweep deigned to come on Monday, as his wife had promised. He arrived at 8.30 a.m. and swept the kitchen chimney. 'Enough said,' wrote Ellen. She also heard from her nephew John. At the time of his writing, he was at the Yeomanry base in Khartoum.

On Tuesday 4 February, Walter was far from well. His liver was out of order and he was dosing himself with camomile tea. On Wednesday, despite the fact that he still felt poorly, Walter got up for dinner. At least, Ellen noted, it was a step in the right direction, but he did not make much of an impact on the dinner that was put in front of him. The dreaded gout had affected Walter's arms during the previous night. He returned to his bed.

There was some better news, though. Kathleen called on her way home to Peopleton with the exiting news that Raymond Wood was expected home 'for good' that night.

The next day, the bitter cold weather continued, the coldest weather for two years. Raymond came in the late morning and stayed to dinner. What a merry dinner they all had. Ellen thought that Raymond looked very well; he was so pleased to be at home again. He went upstairs and had a chat to Walter before he continued on his way to Craycombe Farm. He told them that his brother John, who was out in Egypt, was in hospital again with a chill.

14 February, St Valentine's Day, was far from exciting. The icy grip in the weather continued. Alice went to fetch some margarine from Pershore and get her father some medicine and Walter managed to come downstairs for dinner.

On 15 February, Ellen put a fire in the sitting room where Walter finished making out Mrs Bomford's extremely long bill, thus ending the clerking for 1918. Better late than never.

On the Sunday, it was cold with an east wind. Donald and Ellen got as far as Moor Church in the afternoon, but after that all the family stayed indoors and kept the fire company.

Walter was better and therefore brighter on Monday. It was still cold, and rained 'snow broth' most of the day. Walter spent the time writing and putting his accounts straight. It was too unfavourable for him to venture out the next day, for they all awakened to a white world. Ellen was rewarded by one of the pullets laying an egg. She had a letter from Polly to say that John's chill was in fact malaria but that he was getting better. He sang the praises of the Red Cross, but wished he could get his ticket for Blighty.

Mrs Workman called in the afternoon and gave Alice a very nice hymn book, *Ancient and Modern*, with music that delighted her very much.

Polly suggested that Alice stay with her in Peopleton for a few days the following week, to do some 'little bits of sewing for her'. Alice was not enamoured by this request, but had little option but to oblige.

They heard that the river was flooded in Fladbury. People had to go through Evesham to get to the village of Cropthorne. This meant a nine-mile diversion.

As to the war memorial business, Moor folk thought that having a porch built onto their little church was a good idea. They would erect a memorial tablet inside the porch, inscribed with the names of the men who had served from the village. Inside the church, there would be a tablet with the names of the eight boys who had fallen.

On 26 February, Mrs Pratt came to sell tickets for a social in aid of the War Memorial, which would be held at Moor Village Hall the following Thursday. The next to arrive was Mrs Bancks, asking for refreshments for the coming whist drive – in aid of Fladbury War Memorial.

The following day, Alice returned from 'Pip' in the afternoon, having done all the little jobs of sewing to her aunt's satisfaction.

Ellen sent a black cat kettle holder to her sister-in-law Louise in Wallington for her birthday. She wrote to Edwin and his wife in Malmsbury to wish them well on their fourteenth wedding anniversary.

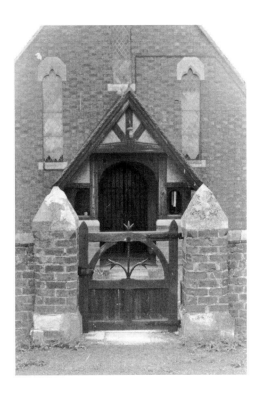

The Memorial Porch, St Thomas' Church, Moor, eventually built in 1923.

The weather was so nice that she ventured into Evesham to buy some woollen vests at Hamilton and Bells for Donald. They had to order them, for they had no woollen ones in stock.

Ellen noted with satisfaction that meat was to be 2*d* per pound cheaper. The mutton that day had cost 1*s* 9*d* per pound.

March came, giving a sample of its cold winds. The family had a letter from Jessie Gibbs in Stourbridge, so Ellen decided to write back and ask her to come and stay.

Donald was eighteen years old on 2 March. Alice gave him a brown leather collar box with four stiff white collars in it. His father gave him a tie in a tie box, and he received a postcard from his Aunt Polly. Donald was now quite grown up. When he went to Pershore to get his hair cut, he also had a shave.

On 3 March, the family had the good news from Hooten Pagnell that Harry Allatt was home, recently discharged from the Royal Flying Corps. He had gone down with the 'flu first, followed by Ethel and Louise. Frank had so far escaped. 'When will it end?' wrote Ellen.

The Spanish 'Flu was causing more deaths than the war. In the neighbourhood, it was very bad again. Edith Haines from Wyre died aged twenty-one. Her death was followed a few days later by the demise of a good mother and wife, Mary Haines, in the prime of life, forty years old. They heard that old Fred Farr had died from the 'flu; and it had also taken Rose Knight, who at thirty-one was young in years but old in suffering. They were both lying dead in the same house. Nearly every home in Moor was affected. Twelve of the people with influenza had attended the whist drive at Fladbury the previous Monday.

Moor Parish Room held a social in aid of their memorial. They hoped to raise £10 with the raffles. All the Gibbs had bought tickets and sociable Donald was going to attend. It was only in the evening, when the family sat down to tea, that Ellen was reminded that it was Shrove Tuesday; she had forgotten all about the pancakes! She promised that she would atone for her neglect next week, when she would have some nice homemade lard.

On Saturday 8 March, it seemed there was the hope of spring in the air. Raymond called on his way to Evesham and came back to Bredon View for dinner and took his mother a piece of pig meat. Raymond complained to Ellen about a sore throat, which filled her with dread. Ellen thought to herself that it was high time that Raymond took a wife who could look after him. He was hoping to take the position of Head Gardener at Craycombe House now that it was being restored as a family home.

On Sunday 16 March, when Ellen returned from Moor Church, she found her 'billet sons' Ben and Edgar at home. They had walked up from their billets in Pershore and stayed to supper. They were loading hay at Pershore Station. They all had a most pleasant evening. The two men entertained them with tales of their experiences since they left Bredon View a year ago.

The following day was a lovely drying day. Ellen got all the washing done – a happy experience that she had not had for months.

On Wednesday morning, Bredon Hill was capped with snow when Ellen awoke. Alice, however, was not deterred from spring-cleaning her bedroom. The weather was worse the following day, with snow and sleet.

21 March may have been the first day of spring, but it did not give that impression to Ellen; when she looked out of her bedroom window in the early morning, the lane was like a brook!

Raymond brightened the gloom of the day when he called in the evening and stayed for a bit of supper. He was now in 'civvies' and looked well. He spoke fondly of Selina, his sweetheart. She was working hard at Wood Norton Hall, where she was acting head housemaid and had little time off.

Saturday dawned to a white world but the snow soon cleared away, although it remained very cold.

Sunday 23 March was the first anniversary of Alice Hodge's wedding. Walter and Ellen went to Fladbury Church; it was a bitterly cold walk across Porters Path.

On 24 March, the hills all around were again white with snow and it was 'bitter'. Ellen had a letter from her nephew John, sent from a convalescent camp near Alexandria. He was taking 'first-class' and hoped soon to be aboard a hospital ship bound for Blighty – the sister ship of the *Titanic*, the marvellous *Olympic*.

On Wednesday, the weather relented. Alice Hodges and Ellen walked up to Throckmorton in the afternoon to call upon the widowed Mrs Rimmell. When they arrived, they found Annie Shenton there; she had cycled over from Pinvin.

Mrs Rimmell talked a great deal about her late husband and was very tearful at times. Annie walked home with them to Bredon View to go home with her husband Tom, who had called in to bring them some garden seeds.

The sweep, known to Ellen as 'Mister Sixfoot', came that morning to sweep the chimneys in the sitting room and their bedroom. There was a great deal of cleaning up to do. Ellen had heard that he had a habit begging for bread and cheese in some households, claiming hunger, but not once did he dare do the same in her household.

Alice and Walter went into Evesham in the afternoon to get a treadle sewing machine and bought a nice Singer for £10. The following day, Mr Clarke brought Alice's sewing machine from Evesham. They found a place in the hall for it to stand and Alice was happy trying it out that evening.

On the last Saturday in March, Walter and Ellen went to Worcester by the 10.00 a.m. train. They found more food in the town now; there was plenty of fish to be had and it was much cheaper. All kinds of sweetmeats and plenty of fruit and meats were available, though they were still dear. There were beautiful American apples at 9d per pound. Oranges were 2d each, or seven for a shilling, and Brazil nuts were 1s 6d per pound.

Ellen bought herself a very pretty hat from Palmers for £1 8d. It was grey with pink chrysanthemums. Walter put the clock back an hour that night ready for summertime the next day.

The next month came in with icy garments and very frosty feet. On Monday 3 April, Alice went into Evesham to get some teeth 'stopped', i.e. filled, but the train was so late that she had to make another appointment for the following Monday. Kathleen agreed to go with her and give her some moral support.

On 2 April, Ellen wrote to Louise Allatt and sent her a box with some lard and brawn.

On Monday 3 April, Corporal Jones called from the German prisoner-of-war camp at Craycombe, where the Prussian prisoners were housed. He called to ask Ellen if she could put up their Commandant and his wife, who were visiting for a week or so. Ellen agreed, so she and Alice busied themselves getting the spare bedroom ready. The next morning, Lieutenant Gamble and his wife arrived. They had travelled from Doncaster, and she was very tired. They seemed to be nice, plain people.

Wednesday 5 April was a memorable day for Ellen, as it was her fifteenth wedding anniversary – and Frank and Ethel Bland's anniversary, too. It was also Kathleen Woods' twenty-first birthday that week, and Donald was going over to her birthday party. Alice intended going, but as usual she backed out, saying that she had a cold and wanted to finish some sewing. Ellen regretted that Alice was not keen on family festivities. Alice seemed uncomfortable in social settings.

On Sunday, Alice got up for early communion, but Ellen could not go, since there were guests in the house. The Lieutenant and his wife were away all day at the camp. They attended Fladbury Church in the evening and they walked home along Porters Path with Walter and Ellen.

On 8 April, Lieutenant and Mrs Gamble left early in the morning. Mrs Gamble was to be put up at the camp for the rest of her visit. Before leaving, she asked Ellen if the Gibbs would put up their daughter at Easter. This time, Ellen did not make any promises.

As it turned out, this was fortuitous, for when Easter did approach, Walter was back in his bed with the dreaded gout, which had developed in his ankle during the night. To make matters worse, he developed sciatica in his hip. The chief nursemaid, Ellen, bathed his foot with hot water, soda, and salt after breakfast, and this seemed to give him some ease for a while.

Louise Allatt had written to thank Ellen for the parcel of 'piggy things'. She told them of the sickness that had returned to their household. Ethel Bland and her husband had been very poorly again.

April saw the family's welcome coal delivery. Harvey Clarke fetched them a ton from Evesham and charged them 6s for haulage, which Ellen thought a shade expensive.

Walter, while not being totally respected in his own home, was certainly a well respected man in the village. Miss Lawson, the Rector's daughter, arrived at Bredon View in a great fluster to find out if Walter was going to the meeting at the Parish Room about the war memorial, as the Rector had suddenly been taken ill. Ellen suspected a heart attack. Walter, though, was still in dreadful pain with his foot. His dutiful daughter Alice rode the three miles into Pershore in the evening to get some medicine for him from the doctor.

Donald went over to the Rectory to enquire after Rector Lawson. He returned to report that he was much better.

Walter had another very bad night, with no rest from the pain. Ellen slept with Alice and rose at 6.00 a.m. in the morning to bathe his foot, but the pain did not ease until the evening. Alice managed to escape in the afternoon when she rode into Pershore to collect their butter ration.

By Saturday, Walter's foot was giving him less pain, but he was very weak after so many sleepless nights.

Palm Sunday was a lovely, bright day. Walter's foot was still hurting and nothing anyone did seemed to bring any relief from the pain.

Norman Bancks came over with his new box camera and took a snapshot of Snip the dog. Ellen began to wonder if the weather was to blame for Walter's painful foot.

Donald was despatched to Fladbury Churchyard that evening to scrub and clean the family gravestones.

Although the next day was windy and showery, Ellen did not mind. Walter's foot was a great deal better and he hoped to get up the following day. Rector Lawson called to see how he was. Ellen thought the Rector looked very 'bad' himself. Donald returned to the churchyard to finish off cleaning the gravestones and to cut the grass.

On Maundy Thursday, Walter's foot was painful again in the night and early morning, so he was still a prisoner to his bed.

Good Friday was a perfect April day, quite the first day of spring. 'A few more days like this and the face of the countryside will be changed,' Ellen wrote.

The next day, Walter was better and hoped to get up, but he could not bear any pressure on his foot.

Donald went to Peopleton that morning to take some daffodils for Ellen's mother's grave, and while he was there he heard the first cuckoo. Ellen had also seen her first butterflies, a yellow one and then a brown one. This meant, according to custom, 'it is white bread for us this year'.

Ellen had been to Fladbury for a portion of the three-hour service and she took some 'daffies' for the graves.

Alas, by Easter Saturday, the dreaded foot was giving Walter more pain and Alice was despatched for some more medicine from the doctor in Pershore. Jimmy Randle came for some old iron that he had bought and he strongly recommended 'Eades Gout Pills'. Jimmy said they always gave him relief, so Walter consented to try them. Donald went off to Evesham to buy him a box.

It was a cold Easter Sunday when Alice and Ellen got up and went to Holy Communion at Moor at 7.00 a.m. Walter, who seemed better, got up to have tea.

Easter Monday was a lovely Bank Holiday, bright and fine all day. Walter got up in the morning; he was better but still had twinges of gout pains about him.

Tuesday was another beautiful day. Walter got up after dinner and was busy going through the church accounts. He found that they were much better than last year, but still in debt.

The following day, Ellen had a postcard from Polly with the good news that John was back in England. He had arrived at Southampton on Sunday morning at 6.30 a.m. and was sent to a military hospital at Halifax. He had his tea at Snow Hill station, Birmingham on Sunday evening. So near and yet so far! He expected to be sent to a hospital in Lincoln.

On the first Sunday after Easter, snowflakes the size of golf balls fell for two hours, bringing back a white world for a while. It was followed by more snow in the night and a sharp frost in the morning. The next day it was still bitterly cold and Walter's gout recurred. He did not get up until dinnertime.

May Day was a lovely warm day and an aeroplane circled around Evesham, flying very low and scattering leaflets promoting cinema films.

Kathleen Woods was poorly again and on Friday 9 May, Walter gave everyone a fright when he had a giddy turn and fell down on the floor as he tried to get up that morning. Ellen fancied that it was his liver.

He went into Pershore in the afternoon to get a tonic made up by Mr Smith, the chemist, who told him he was much too 'low' and must take things easier and 'must live as well as ever he can'.

The weather was getting hotter, so Ellen soon had all her washing dry. The pear and apple trees looked lovely, all of them heavy with blossom.

Despite Walter assuring her that he felt much better, he went off to walk the three miles to Pershore to get himself some 'nourishing' medicine.

The following Sunday, Walter rode on his bike to Fladbury Church, because his foot was so weak and he could not walk. Unfortunately, the ride to church was not without its hazards. Domino, the Dalmatian that belonged to Craycombe House, slipped its lead and chose to bound into the road just as Walter Gibbs reached the crossroads.

There were several very wobbly moments between the dog and the cycle before Walter regained control and continued his journey to church.

Ellen enjoyed a stroll across the sunlit Porters Path. It was pleasant to see the countryside looking so beautiful. Going to church, she could see the distant Cotswolds, Broadway Tower clearly visible. Walking home, she was treated to a long view of Bredon Hill. The majestic Malvern Hills were silhouetted against a crimson and orange sunset. For the first time in years, Ellen felt it was good to be alive. She felt so fortunate to live out her life in the shadow of those glorious hills.

May also saw the beginning of the spring-cleaning. The weather was kind and the slight breeze helped to dry the curtains, valances, and oddments out of their bedrooms. By evening, everything was dry, folded, mangled, and ironed. And Alice was busy getting her summer frocks and petticoats ready for wearing.

On Thursday 22 May, Ellen and Alice began to spring-clean the sitting room. The day was hot, and so was the job.

The gilt pictures were taken down using cotton cloves and gently cleaned. They had to move all the furniture to get the carpet rolled up and out onto the lawn. The furniture was pushed into the middle of the room. Chamois leather, wrung out from a bucket of warm water with a spot of vinegar added, was used to remove the winter grease and grime. The furniture was then covered by dust sheets. The curtains came down to be washed, and the walls and ceilings were brushed with the long-handled bamboo cobweb brush. The windows were cleaned and polished. All the ornaments were removed and washed. It was a full day for Ellen and Alice. It wasn't until the next day that they finished the sitting room to their mutual satisfaction.

The following Saturday, Donald and his father went to Worcester by train. They got Donald a summer-weight suit and paid £5 10s for it. While they were gone, Ellen had a good afternoon sewing; she made herself a summer petticoat for everyday wear.

Typical of local life were the seven little Moor girls, dressed in white with buttercup chains on their heads, and carrying flags and a Maypole, who arrived in the afternoon and treated Ellen to some dancing and singing. They were collecting for the Red Cross.

The weather continued to be very hot. Ellen found it very hard trying to work in the sun and Walter found it difficult to work in the forge. It was more pleasant to work in the evenings.

On Monday 2 June, it was much cooler and Ellen enjoyed picking the first bunch of roses, especially as she had finally finished weeding the large onion bed. John Wood had written to say he was in the Malaria Centre in Lincoln; now much better after a relapse. As fate would have it, he was in the same ward as Sam Perkins, 'from home'. The two men went out as often as they could to see Sam's brother Ben, who was married and lived in Lincoln. They were both made very welcome.

On 7 June, a very hot day, Alice Gibbs turned twenty.

Brother Donald went into Evesham and bought her an autograph book, filling the first page with his own monograph, 'By hook or by crook, I'll be first in this book'. Ellen gave Alice a book by John Oxenham, *Mary-All-Alone*. Aunt Polly gave her some Egyptian pearls that John had sent.

Friday 13 June was a little unlucky, as the wind and rain in the night had blown a lot of plums and apples off the trees and bruised the roses badly. Still, things were not too bad. They heard from Louise and John Aldridge in London. Louise had invited Walter and Donald to visit them, and was delighted that they had finally accepted.

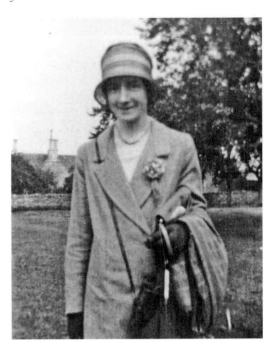

Alice Gibbs.

Father and son set off for London on 14 June by the 11.45 a.m. train; four hours later, they arrived safely at Paddington Station, where John Aldridge was waiting to meet them. Although we don't know from Ellen's diary what they got up to in the city, we do know that they had a great time sightseeing and thoroughly enjoyed themselves, especially Donald. They even postponed the date of their return.

When the wanderers returned home on the evening of 20 June, there was great excitement at Bredon View, for the well travelled men had brought back fancy gifts for their womenfolk. Walter had brought Ellen a lovely bottle of eau-de-Cologne, which was just what she wanted, plus a pretty box. He brought Alice a handbag and mirror, and some Star Sylko cottons that she would find very useful. Donald brought Ellen a 'lucky cat' with the coat of arms of Carshalton on it. For Alice, he had a beautiful little birthday book with quotations from the poet Tennyson. They were 'SO pleased with themselves', wrote Ellen.

Not to be outdone, Ellen decided that she too would like a short break and so wrote to Walter's brother Sidney and his wife Thirza, in Stourbridge, asking if she could pay them a weekend visit. Ellen was always a welcome visitor, it would seem, and was duly invited to stay. Naturally, that would mean leaving everything at Bredon View in tip-top condition, including providing fodder in advance, or 'provender' as Ellen called it, for the family's gastronomic needs.

On Friday 27 June, Ellen wrote in her diary, with some excitement, 'I am off to Stourbridge by the 5.35 p.m. train this evening!' She arrived at Stourbridge Junction at 7.25 p.m. and was met by her nieces, Jessie and Irene. They arrived at Bournville House around 8.00 p.m. Ellen took a stroll around their garden, had supper, and went to bed. This is perhaps not very exciting by modern standards, but for Ellen it was different. And for this hardworking woman, the change was good.

It was cloudy the next morning and much colder, but Thirza and Ellen went shopping and had quite a hunt for potatoes. Old potatoes were then very scarce and cost 2*d* per pound. Ellen was astonished to find that green peas were now 6*d* per pound. Thirza took Ellen along to the church in Stourbridge where she and Sidney were married. After they returned home and had tea, they went by tram to Kinver, where Ellen was taken for a lovely walk along Kinver Edge, beautiful scenery all around.

This quite ordinary day in the lives of these two women who enjoyed simple pleasures turned out to be a quite extraordinary day. As soon as they returned from Kinver, they heard the church bells ringing all around and heard at the Post Office the official news that the peace terms were signed at 3.12 p.m. that day. They felt that it was truly something to thank God for, but it was so sad to think of the children whose fathers would never come home again, and the vast numbers of women left to grieve for sons, husbands, and sweethearts.

Sunday morning, 29 June, was cold and windy. Sidney took them to Wollaston Parish Church. In spite of the weather, it was a beautiful service, opening with the National Anthem and closing with a hymn, 'Now Thank We All Our God'. In the afternoon they visited the War Cemetery and later they went to Bell's Mill, where they had a lovely walk. After a very cold and windy night, the bad weather continued, but at least Ellen knew that all was well back home, for Alice had written to tell her so.

Ellen's visit was nearing its end. She had enjoyed her visit and had a wonderful time, but it was a shame that the weather had been so bad. When she returned home, Ellen was delighted to see her ex-soldier nephew John Wood on the doorstep. He said that he would soon be working in Mr Boucher's Joinery Shop in Pinvin. Much better than living in those horrid hot countries abroad, she wrote.

By Sunday 6 July, the bad weather had passed and it was much warmer. There were special services, thanksgiving for peace, in all the churches in Britain. Mr Parrett took the one at Moor Church; Ellen thought it a good sermon. Poor Walter, however, spent nearly all day in bed, suffering from exhaustion and rheumatic pains. He rallied at teatime and managed to attend Fladbury Church with Ellen in the evening.

On Monday 14 July, Ellen received a postcard from Florrie, written on 24 June, saying that Florrie, Archie, and Bobbie were to embark at Montreal for Liverpool on 6 July. They would be well on their way, Ellen noted with great pleasure. The excitement turned to worry when the *Grampian*, the ship on which they were sailing home, struck an iceberg off Cape Race, Newfoundland. The ship had to return to harbour to be repaired, but all of the passengers were saved. The Albion Line Office confirmed that the passengers were now proceeding to England on the *Empress of Britain*. 'May God Speed that ship!' Ellen wrote with feeling.

On Friday 18 July, there was more 'shipping news': Mr Lewis, Archie's father, had learned from the Albion Shipping Line Office that the passengers on the *Empress of Britain* were expected to land in England on 24-25 July.

On Saturday 19 July, it was the Day of National Thanksgiving and Rejoicing for Peace. There was to be a service at Moor Church taken by the Reverend Parrett. Before the service, there was a jubilant procession around the village, headed by young May Pratt, dressed as the 'Angel of Peace'. Her two attendants, the Atwood girls, were dressed as Britannia and Belgium. There was much waving of flags and patriotic singing. The procession had feasted in Oldham's barn before marching to Moor Church for the religious service at 1.00 p.m. Ellen noted that the church was overflowing.

The congregation stood in hushed silence, awaiting the arrival of the procession. The large congregation had spilled out through the church door, and it proved impossible for poor Alice, sitting at the organ, to see her signal to start playing some impressive entrance music. Suddenly there was a great commotion at the church door, followed by a plaintive wail from the Angel of Peace. She was heard to say, 'Go on in Watty, oh *do* go in!' Ellen turned to see the Angel of Peace and her attendants jostling for position in the open church door, with 'Watty' Clarke and his friends blocking their entrance. Eventually, dignity was restored.

The Angel of Peace adjusted her tinsel tiara and smoothed down her white muslin gown. Aided by her attendants, she was able to progress with dignity up the aisle, with Alice playing a rousing anthem.

The congregation sang the National Anthem followed by the hymns 'Oh God Our Help in Ages Past' and 'Now Thank We All Our God'. Ellen thought that this display was all very well but looked out of place in church.

Towards the end of July, Ellen had a postcard from Polly to say that their niece Florrie Lewis, with her husband Archie and son Bobbie, had landed, of all places, in Glasgow! The *Empress of Britain* could not disembark at Liverpool, owing to the strikers at the Liverpool docks.

It seemed that despite the Representation of the People Act 1918, which had established manhood suffrage and given votes to women over 30 years of age, the unrest that had prevailed among the dockers and other workers before the war was rearing its ugly head again, especially in the north of England. Ellen thought the Russian Revolution had a lot to answer for. The Lewis family hoped to arrive at Norchard House, Peopleton that very day – if the strikers did not prevent them.

Tragedy struck the small village of Moor that July, when young Percy Cotterill was drowned in the river. Locals could only think that he had been taken with cramp, for he was a strong swimmer.

The alarm was raised after a heavy rainstorm burst over the village. His poor mother was frantic and the small population of the village felt dreadful.

When poor Percy's body was recovered from the river, Ellen wrote, 'Ours is a sad little village this day.' Donald showed great compassion when he invited Percy's brothers up to Bredon View' to try to cheer them up.

As with all deaths in the village, one or more of the Gibbs family attended the funeral and Ellen made up a lovely spray of flowers. It was Donald who attended Percy's funeral, where schoolmaster Mr Bancks played the Funeral March and everyone sang Percy's favourite hymn:

> Through the night of doubt and sorrow,
> Onward goes the pilgrim band,
> Singing songs of expectation,
> Marching to the Promised Land.

On the Sunday after the funeral, Donald attended church with Percy's grieving family. Ellen thought that Donald Gibbs was turning into a fine and decent young man with a strong sense of community and duty. She felt that he did things because he wanted to and not because he had to, or was expected to. This was what living in a village meant; people were there for one another with practical or emotional support whenever it was needed. There was always great respect for their dead, whose graves were carefully tended.

The August Bank Holiday was comparatively quiet for Ellen. She used up the last of her spare sugar when she turned 8 lb of prolific plums into jam. She also got her first glimpse of Archie Lewis, home from Canada, when he came over to Bredon View with Will James to have the mare shod. He looked well and little changed. He told Ellen that Canada was much hotter than England in the summer. He promised to return on Sunday with Florrie and Bobbie.

Ellen was very disappointed in early August when her forty-five dozen onions, sent to market a few days earlier, only made a measly 5s! Still, packing up home-grown produce, like apples, plums, onions, and beans, and sending it to market, was a part of Ellen's regular activities; sometimes the returns were good and sometimes they weren't. Coming from a farming family, market gardening was new to Ellen, but fortunately she enjoyed its ups and downs.

On the 'Glorious Twelfth', they heard from Fred Crowther, Walter's nephew from Yorkshire, who wrote to say that he had sent them a box of homemade bread and teacakes. Donald fetched the package from Fladbury Station that evening and the family had some for supper that night. A real treat.

On Saturday 23 August, another lovely day dawned. It was a great day for the city of Worcester, when 9,000 men of the Worcestershire Regiment were to be fêted. They would make a triumphant march through the city. They included many of the village boys; Raymond Wood was among their number.

Towards the end of August, it felt to Ellen more like November, as it was cold and foggy. Still, the jumble sale at the Parish Room, in aid of the Memorial Porch, was well attended and all the rummage was sold in half an hour.

By Monday 1 September, Ellen had finished her plum-picking and everything was ready for Pershore Market. On 4 September, Mrs Workman walked up the lane in the evening and brought Walter 10s towards Moor Church's expenses, as she had made five guineas (£5 5s) at the jumble sale. The price of bread, Ellen noted, was now 9½d for 4 lbs.

On Thursday 4 September, Kathleen Wood came over in the afternoon feeling very pleased with herself, for she had got herself 'a situation' in Worcester looking after two small children, one only a baby. She was to be paid £30 a year and would start on 15 September. She was very excited.

On Saturday evening, 6 September, Walter was busy apple-picking in the paddock when he stopped and went to fetch Ellen. It was to draw her attention to the glorious sunset. Together they stood in the paddock watching the deep scarlet sky creating a backdrop for the darkening Malvern Hills. As much as they worked with and around nature, they never took it for granted and were often in awe of its beauty.

On Friday 12 September, there was another tragedy in the village when Jim Payne, father of Bill and Ernest, both ex-servicemen, had a nasty accident. They heard that he had fallen from a pear tree at Mrs Hemming's up at Hill House in Hill. He had injured himself badly and they had to bring him down to his home in Moor on a dray. The doctor feared that his spine was severely damaged.

By Saturday 13 September, the news about Jim was not good. He was critically ill and the doctor gave his family little hope. He died the next evening. Both Walter and Ellen attended his funeral.

About this same time, Walter also told Ellen that Henry Bancks, Fladbury School's head teacher, had sent in his three months' notice. He had accepted the post of schoolmaster at a larger school in Hampton, Evesham. The Gibbs expressed their sadness at this news but felt happy for the Bancks family.

Also that week, great excitement. The new linoleum arrived for the Gibbs' sitting room floor, but the excitement quickly vanished when Walter discovered that they had not bought enough to cover the whole floor. Oh dear!

He planned to return to Evesham to order some more the next day. When it was finally laid, it looked very nice. Alice and Ellen were busy for the rest of the week tidying up and getting ready for their visitors, Louise Allatt and Frank and Ethel Bland, who were due to arrive on 27 September. Ellen spent a day merrily cooking and cake-making.

27 September was a lovely day as far as the weather was concerned, but the atmosphere at Bredon View was heavy with disappointment. The trains were not running, owing to the railway strike, so of course the expected visitors from Hooten Pagnell in Yorkshire could not travel. Ellen received a wire from them at midday. There had been a lot of bad blood on the railways. Even during the war, there had been several work-to-rule periods when the railwaymen were involved in negotiating their wages. They were still under Government control, but the new pay plan presented to them was so unacceptable that the men had forced a strike.

Monday morning brought a sharp frost that nipped a lot of the flowers, but the rest of the day was beautiful. Ellen noticed a few trains running that day, but the strike was still going on. Walter said that the papers were very against the strike and one paper said of them, 'Like the Germans, we must fight them to the finish.' Ellen heartily agreed. By Tuesday, more trains were running and Miss Willis Bund called in the afternoon to say that she had received a letter from London that morning, so the mail trains were getting through.

The first day of October was dull, cold and wet. Ellen wrote to Louise, Frank, and Ethel to say how very disappointed they all were that their holiday was cancelled.

Walter consoled himself by sending their first load of cider apples to Fladbury Mill to make the first lot of cider, and Alice carried on with her sewing projects, finishing a new nightshirt for Walter and starting a day shirt for Donald.

Saturday 4 October was 'full of sunshine' and Alice went to Moor Church for the afternoon to help decorate for the harvest thanksgiving the next day. Donald took a very large marrow, the largest they had ever grown.

He also took along apples and some fine King Edward potatoes. The offerings were to go to Pershore Cottage Hospital.

There was a good congregation at Moor Church on Sunday afternoon for the Harvest Festival. Alice and Walter attended Fladbury Church for evensong and returned home with the splendid news that the railway strike was over. Despite it being Sunday, Ellen allowed herself a little 'Hurrah-Hurrah' comment in her diary.

On Monday 6 October, the trains were running pretty well as usual. They hoped their Yorkshire visitors would now come to stay, a happy fact that Louise Allatt soon confirmed by letter. Ellen also noted that milk had risen in price to 8*d* per quart.

On Monday 13 October, Walter Gibbs was sixty-two years old. He received a letter from his brother Edwin, a pair of home-made socks from Ellen, tobacco from Donald, and a pair of braces from Alice.

Their visitors finally arrived but the weather was less than kind, with a heavy storm of rain and some hailstones but there was a great deal of happy talking done indoors.

The next day brought a sharp frost; the grass in the garden was quite white. The rest of the day was cold and bright, so their visitors ventured as far as Evesham. They returned with gifts for their hosts: handkerchiefs for Walter; a purse for Alice; a necktie for Donald; and the book *Laddie* by Gene Stratton Porter for Ellen.

When the Yorkshire branch of the family departed, Ellen felt the house was empty of the laughter that had dominated it for the last few days.

On 26 October, the last few German prisoners who worked in the field opposite were leaving the Craycombe camp for home.

Donald walked over to Fladbury to collect his father's boots from Percy Moseley's and he spotted them all at Fladbury station waiting for their special train. Walter's boots were soled and heeled, which cost 7s.

The last of 'Oldham's lot' passed by while the Gibbs were having dinner and Joseph, one of the prisoners that they had befriended, dropped back and waited by the gate. Walter and Donald went out and said goodbye to him; Alice and Ellen waved from the sitting room window. Ellen wondered what he would find when he returned to his family in Austria.

The Germans had been very short of food during the closing years of the war. There was growing discontent among the people, who blamed the German Army's hierarchy for getting it so wrong.

At the beginning of November, Ellen noted that the men coming back from the war were not finding it as easy to get jobs as they would have hoped. Alice Hodges' husband was one of the lucky ones, for he got his job back with the Great Western Railway. Times were tough for these men and their families.

That same week, Ellen invited the grieving Cotterill parents, Jessie and Victor, to tea. It was their last Sunday in Moor before leaving for their new home in Cassingdon near Oxford. Ellen put a fire in the sitting room so they could have some music and enjoy themselves. She hoped that the family would feel happier away from Moor and the tragic memory of young Percy.

On Sunday 9 November, Ellen went on a cold, raw afternoon to Moor Church. Reverend Parret took the service in the extremely chilly church. There was no fire, no coal, and no sexton. Donald rang the church bell and took the collection. Alice and her father went to Fladbury, so they did not return home blue with cold like Ellen and Donald.

On 11 November, there was a very sharp frost, followed by a glimmer of sunshine. Fladbury and Moor, like the rest of the country, observed the two-minute silence at 11.00 a.m., the time the armistice was signed the year before. It was a most solemn two minutes, thinking of the fallen.

Donald had gone down to Moor Church to ring the bell a few minutes before 11.00 a.m., and Ellen heard the hooters from Springhill and maroons from the river sounding all around. Throughout the whole of Britain, everyone stood in utter silence, in memory of those men and women who did not return home.

Wednesday 12 November brought the first snow, but Alice bravely struggled into Pershore to fetch the butter and bravely struggled back home again. Walter's cold was a little better and he decided to rise from his bed for dinner. 'Heaven be praised!' wrote Ellen. He was not well enough to venture outside, as it was so bitterly cold. He didn't feel like working in his forge, but he did help the family pack a few boxes of apples.

On Friday 14 November, there was a brief period of sunshine. Rector Lawson called that evening with a novelty sweet for Ellen to taste; it was four chocolate marshmallows and 'very nice they were too!' she wrote.

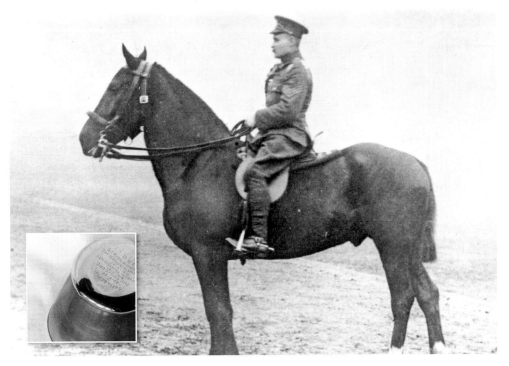

Captain Bomford and Bob the horse, who served together in France 1916-18. *Inset:* Bob's preserved silver hoof.

The next day, Saturday, was very cold again Walter dealt with the church heating apparatus at Fladbury Church to make sure the congregation would be warm the following day.

On Sunday 16 November, Ellen went down to Moor Church at 11.00 a.m. to start the fires in the stoves, which was no easy job. She was determined that the congregation would not freeze again that afternoon during the service.

There were two coal stoves either end of the small church. When the wind was blowing in a certain direction, one stove was prone to give out clouds of smoke. But when the wind changed, the other stove would start to smoke. Ellen soon found herself rushing from one stove to the other with a shovel full of burning coals, enveloped in smoke. Folk would sometimes mutter, unkindly, ''Er does that to keep the Parson w-a-a-rm'.

Alice and Donald went to Fladbury in the evening but Walter and Ellen kept the fire company at home and had a nice quiet read.

The following Tuesday was a long one and a busy one. Annie's husband Tom Shenton called. Just as he was going at 9.00 p.m., who should call but Mr Alfred Bomford? He finished up the evening well. He did not go until 10.30 p.m!

He told them that his nephew Captain James Bomford was now home for good. On his way home, James decided to go to Aldridge's Sale Yard in London and buy his horse, Bob; both horse and rider had come through the war unscathed. He could not resist also buying Lassie, who happened to be for sale as well. She was a high-spirited Welsh horse who had belonged to the Colonel of his battalion. James boarded his train at

Paddington Station for home and the following day the two horses arrived in Fladbury by horsebox to begin their peacetime existence. He used to ride the horses around the fields and some of his workforce would know if he was in a good humour or not by the way he rode; 'Jimmy be tearin' up the sprouts agin!' they would mutter.

From 1914, Bob had served in France with the 2/8th battalion of the Worcestershire. He would die in Springhill in March 1939, at the age of twenty-nine.

The late night with Alfred Bomford must have set back Walter's cold, for he spent the next day in his bed.

The third week in November proved quite exciting for Donald. He had his first shave with a cut-throat razor and only managed to cut himself a little. 'Mind you', Ellen wrote, 'he nearly shaved his face away!'

Monday 24 November 1919 was a lovely bright day for Ellen's fifty-fourth birthday and Polly's sixty-first birthday. Naturally, they spent the day together. Polly was very pleased with her gift from Alice. It was a 'victory and peace' cushion. Florrie gave Ellen a small tray cloth and Raymond presented her with the dessertspoon that had stayed with him all the time he was in Belgium, France, and Italy. John gave her his teaspoon from his time spent in Egypt. Donald gave her a bottle of lavender water and Alice promised to buy her the book of her choice the next time she went into Evesham. By Tuesday, it was back to reality and Ellen got on with drying the clothes.

On 27 November, it was such a dull, dark day that Ellen decided to go into Evesham to get some wool to knit herself some stockings and a few other things. The price of wool was staggering: 7¼d per ounce! She was late getting back and she was mightily pleased that Walter met her at the station with a lantern, for it was a pitch-black night to stumble along the mile-long Porters Path on her own.

On 28 November, it was dull and cold again, but Walter felt well enough to work at the forge, so Ellen did some letter writing. The next day, Ellen woke to a snowy world and it continued to snow throughout the day, although it was quite slippy underfoot.

On Advent Sunday, there was a very sharp frost in the morning. Walter was called up early to roughen the shoes of the milkman's horse before he could go on his rounds.

On 2 December, after a lot of rain and wind in the night, the snow was banished and a lovely drying day dawned, with beautiful sunshine. The next day it was raining, cold, and windy, which was unfortunate, for on that day the new farmers' market was opened at Pershore Station by Lord and Lady Coventry. His Lordship sold the first pot of apples, which made £25, since they were sold over and over again, to raise money in aid of the Pershore Cottage Hospital. The ever-changing weather threw up a gale during the proceedings.

Mr Arthur, the new schoolmaster of Fladbury School, called in the afternoon to see Walter about business. Ellen went into the sitting room to speak to him; he seemed a pleasant, gentlemanly man with 'no side'.

On Saturday 6 December, Ellen prepared to cross swords with her friend the sweep. The 'Knight of the Brush' arrived at 10.30 a.m., having been timed to come at 9.00 a.m. He swept the kitchen chimney, so they were at least smoke-free. Donald, meanwhile, battled his way into Evesham in a sharp storm of hailstones to have his hair cut at the extortionate price of 8d. Ellen only paid a penny more to have the chimney swept.

On the second Sunday in Advent, the weather displayed both wind and heavy rainstorms; fortunately it was a lovely moonlit night when Ellen accompanied Donald to Fladbury Church that evening for his first appearance as a member of the choir.

Alice stayed at home with her father. The following Monday it was cold but bright, so Ellen washed out the woollen things, while Walter found himself doing something a little more pleasurable – making his last seventy gallons of cider at Fladbury Mill. That evening, however, Ellen had the great satisfaction – after all those terrible war years and shortages – of making a decent quantity of Christmas mincemeat.

Wednesday brought more peacetime cheer when a box arrived from Fred Crowther containing teacakes, a plum pudding, and two cakes. Ellen served one of the cakes for tea – a wonderful treat for all of them.

On Saturday 13 December, the local MP, Commander Eyres-Monsell, unveiled the War Memorial at Fladbury at 1.45 p.m. The Gibbs family gathered, with the people from the two villages of Fladbury and Moor, for a most moving ceremony. It commenced with the singing of the hymn, 'Oh God Our Help in Ages Past', followed by a thanksgiving and prayers from Rector Lawson. It concluded with the National Anthem. Commander Eyres-Monsell spoke very well, and so did Mr Francis from The Brooklands, Fladbury; he had lost a son in the war. Afterwards, the villagers stood quietly reading the long list of names on the Memorial. Ellen's heart went out to the folk who read the name of a loved one; one who would never return home to them. The Gibbs family walked home quietly, along Porters Path, keeping their sad thoughts to themselves.

The following day, Walter was not feeling well, so doom and gloom descended upon Bredon View once more. Ellen deduced that his liver and stomach were out of order. He did not go out all day. Ellen escaped to Moor Church in the afternoon and Donald and Alice went over to Fladbury for evensong.

By Thursday 18 December, Ellen was busy writing her Christmas letters.

On Friday 19 December, she noted that the engraved Memorial Tablet had been fixed in Moor Church. That would have meant a great deal to Moor folk.

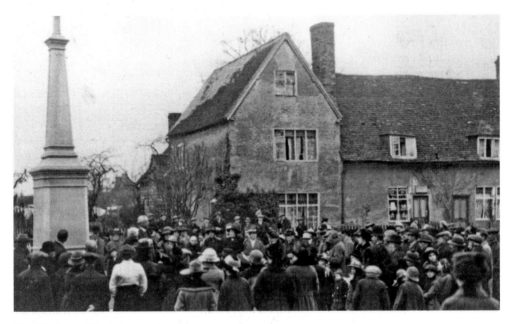

The Fladbury War Memorial.

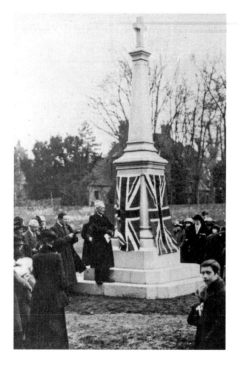

The dedication service for the Fladbury War Memorial.

On the fourth Sunday of Advent, Rector Lawson dedicated the Memorial Tablet at Moor Church. The Gibbs family attended and despite it being stormy, there was a good congregation. It was yet another occasion to mourn the dead and pray that their lives were not given in vain. Despite this terrible sacrifice of young lives, there was not a feeling of peace in the land, Ellen noted. There were not the jobs the men expected after the war and there was a great deal of unrest. She hated to even think that the war years might, in the end, be wasted years, especially for the ones who went to fight.

On 23 December, Ellen noted with a great deal of satisfaction that she had made four plum puddings. The puddings were boiling merrily away in the afternoon when Rector Lawson called and begged a cup of tea. Ellen suspected that the Rector was a secret admirer of her culinary skills, for she had fed and watered him on many occasions. Whenever he was in the vicinity, he always called in for some of Ellen's wholesome fare. Today, the Rector was on top form and treated the family to some recitations from the works of Rudyard Kipling, much to the embarrassment of Alice, who disliked such a show of emotion at such close quarters.

On the day of Christmas Eve there was lovely sunshine – a good drying day for Ellen, thank goodness. She went down to Moor Church soon after breakfast to lay the fire in the stoves. The rest of the day she was busy with mince pies and cakes and general food preparation. The family decided to give each other their presents that evening.

Ellen had five shillings from Walter, a lovely calendar from Donald, and a book, *Down Our Street* by J. E. Buckrose, from Alice.

Christmas Day arrived with rainstorms, but Ellen didn't mind. She was busy enjoying some decent Christmas cooking for the first time in years. Alice laid the table and then

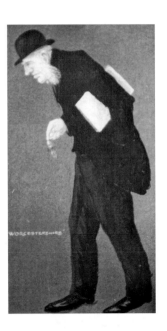

Caricature of Mr Willis Bund.

departed for Holy Communion at Moor while Donald went to the service at Fladbury. The blot on the horizon was Walter. His cold was worse, as was his indigestion, so he could not do justice to his Christmas dinner. He did not accompany the rest of the family to Moor Church in the afternoon, when the congregation were swept along in a rousing service taken by Mr Willis Bund.

The intimidating Mr Willis Bund, KC, CBE, JP, always made a dramatic entrance. The tall, thin, be-whiskered gentleman would stride down the aisle with his preaching gown billowing in his wake. Once he was at the lectern, he would kick away the stool that lesser mortals used to get a better view of the congregation – sometimes with such force that the stool would rebound from the wall and bounce down the altar steps. He peered down his aquiline nose to glimpse at his notes, and then he would announce the number and loudly recite the first verse.

The little church would reverberate with his chosen text followed by a sermon delivered to a spellbound congregation. If the congregation were not God-fearing when they entered the church, Mr Willis Bund made certain that they were God-fearing when they meekly filed out. The closing carol gave everyone time to recover before they quietly filed past him, out of church, humbly muttering Christmas greetings to this ruler of Worcestershire.

For the rest of the day, the Gibbs family had a quiet evening at home with some music and a few games of ludo. Rather dull and disappointing, Ellen wrote, owing to Walter being poorly. She cheered herself up, however, when she counted the record amount of Christmas greetings that they had received by post over the last few days.

On Boxing Day, there were more Christmas missives. Walter was a bit brighter and had started his clerking. Both children fled the nest: Alice set off for Peopleton and Donald to Hampton to see the Bancks family. Both had a wet ride home to tea.

The next day, a great storm of wind, hail, and rain swept across the country. After it had passed, it was fine and bright for the remainder of the day, but very windy. Annie and Tom Shenton were expected to tea but did not turn up. Ellen was uncertain if it was because of the weather or yet another of their domestic disputes.

On the first Sunday after Christmas Ellen arose early on a cold, frosty morning to attend Holy Communion at Moor Church and to light the stoves for the rest of the services. Reverend Parrett came over to help. The Rector was not very well, so he took both services that day.

It rained very fast as they came out of church, and it continued to rain for the rest of the day. Only Donald ventured along Porters Path to Fladbury in the evening.

The next day was fine and Alice and Ellen tackled the washing together and prepared for the pig killing the next day. Walter arose and went down to the doctor's that morning to get himself some medicine for 'disordered stomach and liver'. The Gibbs family continued with their ordinary, busy lives.

As the New Year approached, Ellen sat by the fire in the sitting room and took a quiet few moments thinking of the past and the future.

They had survived four years of war and the terrible influenza epidemic. The young men that she truly cared about had come through the war unharmed, for which she was truly thankful. Although many of the men were lost and would walk no more on Bredon Hill, it appeared that the world she knew had changed little on the surface.

She did have a vote and that pleased her. But it was, in reality, a man's world, and it would be many years before women's opinions were taken seriously. A better education for women was essential, Ellen thought to herself. It was not a waste, as many men thought. The war had liberated many women out of sheer necessity, but now it was back to the home and the care of children. Many of the women who had lost their men in the war would be deprived of any such fulfilment.

In many ways, Ellen felt fulfilled, despite the fact that most of her family were hers by adoption. She was a good wife to Walter, but she had always known that she was not the love of his life. She felt that he respected her and despite his many outside obligations they did enjoy a companionship that grew with the years.

Despite his hypochondria Walter was a fit man; hopefully he would continue to work in the forge for the foreseeable future. Donald, she feared, would not necessary follow in his father's footsteps. He showed little interest in his father's work, but loved working on their land. He was a willing young fellow, always ready to help, but he lacked the drive or ambition that his father had.

They relied heavily upon Springhill for most of their work, but young Captain Bomford was a new broom at Springhill and he might well want to establish his own blacksmith's shop there.

Donald, she felt, was a real son to her; he gave her a great deal of pleasure. Ellen knew that she would never enjoy the deep love of a daughter, but Alice was a dutiful girl and a good companion. She showed no inclination to marry apart from one youthful crush, which Walter had smartly squashed, considering it not a suitable match.

Walter would have to look to Donald to produce the next family of Gibbs to live in Lower Moor. Ellen feared that there was no guarantee that he would stay in the village. She hoped that she was wrong and that with the Lord's help that things would work out favourably.

Afterword

Walter Gibbs died in 1931, leaving Ellen to watch over the decline of their business and the sale of the house. Ellen and Alice moved into Whytes Orchard at the end of Blacksmiths Lane. Captain Bomford established a blacksmith's shop at Springhill. In 1933, Ellen died of breast cancer.

Donald Gibbs married and went to live in Evesham between the wars. He had a daughter, Margaret.

Alice played the organ at Moor Church for over fifty years, She continued with her exquisite sewing, creating many vestments for the churchs. On her sitting room wall was the framed family tree that she was so proud of. It was a blessing that she was able to express herself through her music and literature. During the Second World War, she was forced to work in a fruit-canning factory in Wyre. She did, however, enjoy the company of several land girls billeted with her when they were working at Springhill. She read a great deal and listened to her radio. The one time of day when you were wise not to visit Alice Gibbs was when *The Archers* was being broadcast.

In the Second World War, most of the men in the parish declined to rush forward to save king and country. They had done enough in the First World War. Many of them made a good living out of horticulture and agriculture instead.

Elizabeth Smyth of the Manor House became a widow. Her beloved son, now Major Montague Smyth, had been missing since the fall of Singapore. The men of Fladbury village established a Volunteer Fire Service in the Manor House's coach house. Every evening, Elizabeth would see that the men had enough firewood to light a fire and enough fresh cold water to make tea.

When she died, she did not know that her beloved son Monty was alive and a Japanese prisoner of war. The men of the Volunteer Fire Service gently carried her coffin up the path to Fladbury Church for the burial service. Her grave is just outside the church door. That way, the village folk said that she could see what was going on; such was their affection for the lady.

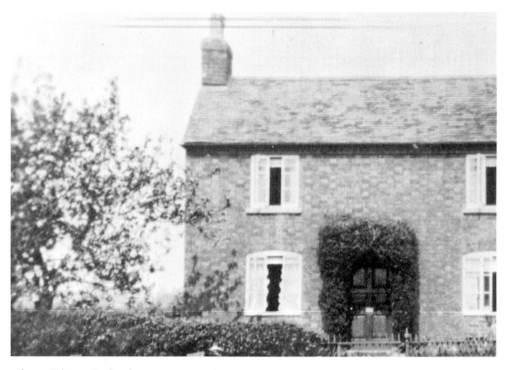

Above: Whytes Orchard.

Below: Alice, Ellen, Donald, and Walter, several years after the end of the war.

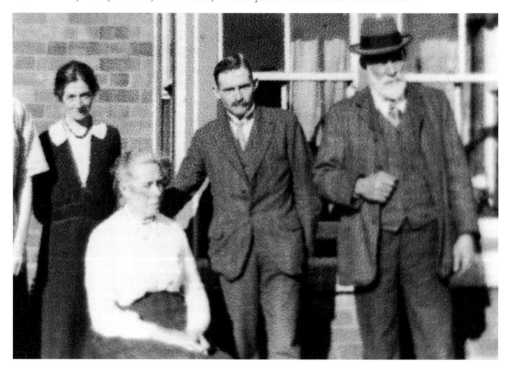

Notes

One sieve is a basket equivalent to half a bushel. A bushel contained 40 lb of apples.

A pot was made of willow and was shaped like and inverted beehive. A half-pot held 22 lb of gooseberries.

Since the end of the First World War, many people have lived at Craycombe House, among them Francis Brett Young, a popular author. He had several staff quarters pulled down. Was it because of the ghost?

I spoke to the gardener's boy when he was a very old man and he very reluctantly, after a lot of prodding, said that he had seen the girl in white at Craycombe.

One summer evening my husband and I took the letter from Viscount Cobham telling me about the ghost up to Craycombe. I met the then-owner, a Mr Daws. We talked a while and he suggested that we walk down to the orangery and the lake. I can tell you now that I have never experienced such a weird, fearful feeling. My manners completely left me and I quickly climbed back up the bank, towards the house. When we were gathered there, I was very glad to accept a stiff drink.

Acknowledgements

I owe Carole Wale a great deal, for without her constant encouragement and valuable assistance I would not have persevered with this book. And without Philip Killeen's wizardry with my computer and Alex Killeen's constant help, I would not have survived.

I would like to thank Christopher and Corah Carney for their support, Grace Judge née Gibbs, who generously lent me family photographs and contributed valuable family information, and the late Mrs Eleanor Savery, who allowed me to read the wartime school log written by Mr Bancks. She also granted me access to the *Fladbury Parish Magazine*, written by Rector Lawson.

I am also grateful to Mike Izod, who generously provided many valuable photographs of Fladbury from his collection, Mrs Beatrice Mills of Lower Moor, who contributed and checked valuable village information, the late Major Montague Smyth, who loaned me family photographs, the late 'Mame' Mansell for stories of Fladbury School during the war, the late Selina Wood, who told me all about Wood Norton before and during her service there, Marion Bomford, for her prompt assistance whenever I called upon her, and Mrs N. Thomas, for her patience in helping me with the Payne family history.

Linda Statye of Lower Moore double-checked numerous facts for me. I.C. Wallace of the Leeds Postcard Collection gave me permission to use the Great War postcards. The late Alan Langman related his First World War experiences to me and also checked all the horticultural details in the manuscript.